Ten Secrets
of
Overcomers

True Stories of Triumph

by

Anne Kleehammer

"In this world you will have trouble.
But take heart! I have overcome the world."
John 16:33 (NIV)

Copyright © 2014 Anne Kleehammer
All rights reserved.

ISBN: 0692298932
ISBN 13: 9780692298930

Acknowledgements

I extend a huge thank you to my ten overcomers for their willingness, availability, and enthusiasm to be interviewed for this book. You trusted me to give voice to your experiences. I'm inspired by your deep desire to help others by telling your life story. Thank you to Stacy Cleveland, Eric Gibson, Josh Hamilton, Lisa Ann Hammond, Debbie Lee, Bob Mortimer, Gigi Murfitt, Dr. Hejal Patel, Bernie Salazar, and Phyllis Vavold.

During the long process of interviewing, writing, and publishing I was covered in prayer by faithful friends and family. You encouraged me and kept me going! Thank you to Cara Ayer, Sheila Craw, Brett and Joy Farley, George and Georgia Farley, Janine George, Frank Giggans, Maureen Godfrey, Carmen Gorak, James and Wendy Haslim, Nancy Keller, Derek Kleehammer, Thomas Kleehammer, Kirk Kraft, Pat Krell, Kim Martinez, Sharon Megahee, Jeanne Farley Rodgers, Julia Sapek, Sandy Shuts, Kathy Thompson, and Kristine Vernon-Cole.

Thank you to Diana Savage, Savage Creative Services, for thorough editing and helpful comments. Thanks to David Sanford who gave me editorial direction in the early stages of this book. A special thanks to Dave Ryan and Sarah Kleehammer for critiques and unique vision. Thank you to my husband, Tom, who acted as my first proofreader and adviser.

I'm grateful to God for the many lessons he taught me during this publication process and for how he will work in the lives of each person who reads this book.

TABLE OF CONTENTS

INTRODUCTION

What motivates people to overcome their problems? What compels them to take on challenges and succeed while others stumble and lose their way? What are the secrets of being an overcomer?

I've always been captivated by these questions, so I started collecting life stories of those who had overcome big challenges in their lives. I read biographies, newspaper articles, magazines, online sites, and pursued recommendations of family and friends. My passion for finding answers pushed away my fear of asking for personal interviews with real-life overcomers.

With each interview and life story, I glimpsed a unique personality who grabbed hold of certain qualities, or "secrets" to overcome their problems. What a goldmine I discovered! These stories of conquering circumstances *need* to be told because we can learn from these overcomers.

If life is crashing down on you, or if you find yourself in a deep valley with no way out, or if you're just experiencing a bump in the road, read these life stories for motivation and encouragement. They are the histories of men and women like you who overcame what seemed like insurmountable obstacles. Each person faced a different set of circumstances, disabilities, and even diseases, but dug deep inside to change direction. Not only did they overcome, but they also helped others by using what they learned from their life experiences.

We can unlock the secrets that helped them succeed. I promise you, their wisdom will deeply impact you, as it has me. Think of these overcomers the next time you face adversity, and ask yourself how they would have handled it.

When life seems to crush you, think of Debbie Lee's courage to turn her son's death into a life's work speaking out for our troops and helping families of the fallen.

When you feel overwhelmed, think of Bob Mortimer missing both legs and an arm but remaining optimistic, humorous, and steadfast in his faith and trust in God.

Remember that you don't need to have Tourette Syndrome to learn from Lisa Ann Hammond's courage to give her testimony and sing to audiences while all her symptoms are on display.

You don't have to be diagnosed with cancer to be uplifted by Dr. Hejal Patel's example to fight your battles and never give up.

When you face grief or any kind of tragedy and want to wallow in your pain, choose to do something positive and trust in God's provision as Phyllis Vavold did.

Look to Bernie Salazar who gained inner confidence and a positive attitude in his weight-loss journey, and hear him say "You're worth being healthy!"

Remember Stacy Cleveland "taking off her mask and being real," when she surrounded herself with accountability partners and leaned on God's strength to overcome her addiction and homelessness.

When you tire of trials in life, recollect Eric Gibson's struggles with a spinal-cord injury that put him in a wheelchair and take note of how he thinks of his injury as a blessing.

When you're weary and want to give up, think of Gigi Murfitt trusting in God for the strength to get through another day of being the legs, arms, and cheerleader for her disabled son.

Even if you're not struggling with a drug addiction, you can be inspired by Josh Hamilton's honest and humble assessment of himself and his need for God's help.

Learn that overcoming is not a single act, but an ongoing process. It requires getting up every day and tackling what's before you. Disease, loss, physical disabilities, drug addiction, emotional snares, and negative attitudes are conquered one day at a time, one step at a time.

Let the voice of each overcomer speak to you. Listen to the inspiration and apply each lesson to your own life. Be encouraged! Be inspired! Be an overcomer!

CHAPTER 1

SECRET NUMBER ONE: BE COURAGEOUS

THE STORY OF DEBBIE LEE

When Debbie Lee unwrapped one of the presents at her surprise birthday party, she found an Angel of Courage statue.

The friend who'd given her the gift said, "You remind me of such a woman of courage with all you've been through in your life and how you stay positive in your faith!"[1]

At the small-group Bible study hosting the party, little did anyone know how much additional courage Debbie would need that August night.

While everyone finished cake and ice cream, Debbie's cell phone rang.

"Hey Mom, where are you?" asked Kristofer, Debbie's oldest son.

"I'm at my small group Bible study. Why?"

"How long will it take you to get home?" he pressed.

"Oh, five minutes, maybe seven. Why? What's up?"

"You need to come home," Kris said.

Debbie felt troubled. She grabbed her purse and told everyone, "Please be praying. Something isn't right."

Driving home, her mind focused on her youngest son, Marc, twenty-eight and a US Navy SEAL,[2] recently deployed to Iraq. She thought, *What's going to face me at home?*

She sang a Christian song "I Put My Hope" to calm herself.

When she turned onto the street where she lived in Surprise, Arizona, she saw Kris pacing the sidewalk.

"Mom, the Navy's here," he said.

She began to cry. "No, no!" She knew if Marc had been injured, military representatives would call, not come to her home.

Two Navy officers dressed in crisp, white uniforms, one a tall chaplain and the other a woman Casualty Assistance Calls Officer (CACO), met her inside.

"We can tell by being in your home that you're a woman of faith," one of them said. "You're going to need to rely on your faith for what we have to say. Your son, Marc Alan Lee, has been killed in action."

The words crushed Debbie like an overpowering wave. She couldn't breathe. She was sinking, drowning in pain. But even then, she felt God holding her.

"I could feel God's presence," she said later. "I knew he was with me. I knew this would be the toughest thing in my life, but I had confidence that he would get me through it. I knew God would walk beside me; he would carry me when I needed to be carried. He would embrace me when I needed to be held."

The Navy officers lingered for a while, then Debbie's small group friends, who had followed her home after waiting for some time, gathered around her. They cried with her, prayed, and talked about Marc. As night crept into morning, everyone left, and Kris went to sleep. Debbie opened her Bible to Psalm 27. She read, "The Lord is my light and my salvation; Whom shall I fear? The Lord is the strength of my life; Of whom shall I be afraid?"[3]

Debbie cried out, "God, just take me away, hide me, protect me!"

Then she read:

"For in the time of trouble He shall hide me in His pavilion; In the secret place of His tabernacle He shall hide me...Wait on the Lord; Be of good courage, and He shall strengthen your heart; Wait, I say, on the Lord!"[4]

Oh Lord, there's that courage theme again, she thought.

Later as she reflected on that night she said, "I was crying in pain, but also in peace. God was right there with me saying, 'I'll protect you, honey, I'll save you. Here, come into my arms.'"

Today, Debbie Lee still grieves the death of her son, Marc, on August 2, 2006, the first Navy SEAL to be killed in Iraq. The pain of losing a child doesn't go away; it remains deep and raw. But Debbie pushed through her pain and changed her loss into a positive force. She uses every opportunity to promote and support military troops, crossing the United States on speaking tours, and she has given over a thousand media interviews. She turned her heartbreak into a life's work of helping the families of fallen and wounded warriors through her nonprofit organization America's Mighty Warriors.

No Stranger to Adversity

Marc's death was not the first time Debbie Lee faced adversity in her life. Her first husband, the father of her three children, had abused her so much that he almost killed her. After the divorce she struggled as a single mother with small children. She underwent surgery for uterine cancer at age twenty-eight. And just when things seemed to stabilize with a second marriage, her husband committed suicide. Debbie was only thirty-nine when she became a widow.

She says, "I had been through so many trials and tragedies in my life, but it was God using those to prepare me for some of the toughest days of my life when we found out Marc had been killed. If I had not been through all those trials, I wouldn't have been strong enough to withstand it."

Naming Marc

At twenty-three and just divorced, Debbie already had a three-year-old son and an eighteen-month-old daughter when she found out she was pregnant again. She had no child support and no help from family, so for a time she worked three jobs to support her children.

On March 20, 1978, in Portland, Oregon, Debbie delivered her third child, a boy. Debbie expected to stay in the hospital for three days, but a nurse hurried into her room one day after the delivery. "We need your hospital bed, so we're sending you home. Before you go, you need to name the baby," she said abruptly.

Debbie glanced at the menu on her tray table. The date *March* was on it, but the *h* was covered up. She saw *Marc* and liked it as a name. She didn't know at the time that *Marc* meant *Mighty Warrior*. She now believes it was God's way of telling her Marc's purpose in life.

4

Her Surrender

A few years later, Debbie fell, injured her back, and for three months could only lie in bed, unable to move. The total dependence and helplessness forced her to evaluate her life. Although she had grown up in a Christian home and went to church regularly, she had no sense of a relationship with God. Broken, she admitted her life was in shambles. At age thirty, she gave up control and offered her life to Christ. "I don't have much, but what I have is yours," she whispered.

"I always thought God would make me a mamsy-pamsy, no-backbone kind of person!" she explained later.

When she learned God had created her with a strong-will to be used for him, not in rebellion, she was amazed and sorrowful at the same time. "Are you kidding me? All those years I fought him, I dishonored him, and grieved him by the choices I had made. I was so sorry and so repentant, and he forgave me!"

Shortly after that experience, Debbie felt God urging her to open a Christian preschool and kindergarten in Hood River, Oregon, where she lived. For fifteen years she directed and taught at Kids R Us while she also homeschooled her children.

Marc's Childhood

Debbie describes Marc as a happy child, with a perpetual goofy sense of humor and a caring attitude toward others. He was voted Class Clown in high school, and he excelled at soccer. Even though he had never played soccer as a child, his lack of skills didn't stop him in high school. Determined, he spent hours dribbling the ball, doing headers, and dedicating himself to learning the game. The coach he had his freshman year later confessed that Marc had been one of the worst soccer players he'd ever seen. Later, Marc was named Most Improved Player, became the youngest soccer coach at his high school, played on the Master's College team in Los Angeles, and joined several Hispanic leagues in Oregon. His talent in soccer led him to try out with the Colorado Rapids, a professional soccer team, but the night before tryouts, he injured his knee, requiring surgery.

Debbie watched his dream die. Recovering at home, Marc read about the Navy SEALs in a biography. While he strengthened his knee, he researched what it took to be a SEAL. The dream of living the life of a warrior tugged at his heart. In May 2001, he boldly walked into a US Navy recruiter's office and signed a contract with an option to train for the SEAL teams.

SEAL Training

After Navy basic training, Marc began his Basic Underwater Demolition/SEAL (BUD/S) training, known as one of the toughest military programs in the world. Pushed beyond physical limits and relying on mental stamina, three out of four men quit before they finish. Marc trained for hours in the frigid Pacific Ocean off Coronado, California. Sometimes his team hauled three-hundred-pound logs in and out of the pounding surf. Every day they were ordered to get "wet and sandy." Fully dressed, including combat boots, they hurled themselves into the ocean, rolled in the gritty sand, then ran for miles. He tackled the infamous obstacle course, climbing ropes and walls and scrambling up and down a cargo net as high as a four-story building. Unfortunately, Marc fell ill with pneumonia and pulmonary edema and was pulled from training. He entered the next class, and although he chose to "ring the bell" and quit, the tenacious and determined Marc came back to graduate in March 2004, placing second in his class and becoming an "elite warrior."

Debbie's oldest son was a Marine, so when she learned about the intensity of Marc's SEAL training she said, "I didn't want my boys to be pansies or wimps, but maybe I went overboard just a little!"

The Battle in Ramadi, Iraq

In 2006, Marc deployed to support Operation Iraqi Freedom with SEAL Team 3. The team's mission was to seek out and eliminate insurgent strongholds in the heart of downtown Ramadi. On every reconnaissance, Marc carried the big machine gun, an M-60, without a shoulder strap in the intense 115 to 120-degree heat.

The Navy representatives, along with Marc's teammates, told Debbie about Marc's last day on August 2, 2006. From a rooftop, SEAL Team 3 had fought one of the fiercest battles in Iraq. The firestorm raged for two hours. Bullets pounded like hail. Shrapnel hit one teammate in the head. As others knelt to help him, Marc stood in the direct line of fire to provide cover as a medic rushed to the rooftop. Marc fired nonstop. Rock steady. Fearless. Highly trained. When the injured teammate had to be evacuated, Marc stood in the line of fire for a second time so all of his teammates could descend safely from the roof.

The SEAL team returned to base only to learn that more insurgents were attacking.

"Are you up to going back out?" the chief asked.

"Roger that. Let's go get 'em!" replied Marc.

Back in downtown Ramadi, they cleared houses one by one. As Marc led his team up the stairs of one house, bullets zinged at them through a window. For the last and final time, Marc turned into the gunfire and willingly gave up his life.

"To get the enemy to focus on you is pretty selfless," Debbie says. "He didn't weigh the pros or cons. He knew it was the right thing to do—for his buddies, for you, for me, and for this nation."

The Navy SEAL camp in Ramadi has been named after Marc Alan Lee since his death. He was awarded the Silver Star, Bronze Star with Valor, Purple Heart, and Combat Action Ribbon, as well as having a training center on the Naval Amphibious Base in Coronado, California, dedicated to him.

HER MISSION

Just weeks after Marc's death, Debbie had her "marching orders" to encourage the family of Mike Monsoor, a Navy SEAL also in Iraq, who threw himself onto a grenade to shield his team from the blast. In addition, she felt called to greet Marc's teammates as they arrived home in Coronado. Marc had tried to explain the intense brotherhood of his SEAL teammates, but Debbie hadn't understood. However, as she spent time with the men and realized how much they loved Marc and grieved his death, her eyes were opened. Now she feels like she's adopted a bunch of boys who are Marc's brothers. "Marc's final gift to me was his teammates."

She often gets calls and e-mails from SEALs. "Hey, Mama Lee, how're ya doing?" they ask.

"It's a badge of honor for these guys to consider me like their mama," Debbie says.

Supporting the Troops

Debbie Lee joined a cross country bus tour to support the troops. At the first stop, without any warning, she was introduced to speak.

"Here with us is the mother of a fallen Navy SEAL, Marc Lee. She's going to speak."

So Debbie, terrified to speak in front of people, held the microphone with both hands to keep it from shaking. At every stop after that, she continued to speak about Marc's heroic actions and her deeper understanding of the great personal sacrifices made for this country's freedom. Now, a fearless and powerful speaker, she continues to champion Marc's fight for freedom. To date, she's been on so many speaking tours that she's lost count.

Debbie Lee became the first Gold Star[5] Mom in history to visit the place where her son was killed. In 2007 and again in 2010, she went to Ramadi, Iraq, saw Camp Marc Alan Lee, and walked where her son had walked.

On her 2007 trip, she handed out thousands of Christmas cards and care packages to the troops in Iraq. She did the same in 2008 at Guantanamo Bay Naval Base, Cuba.

Currently, Debbie Lee appears on Capitol Hill to advocate for military funding, Rules of Engagement (ROE), and a congressional gold medal for Tyrone Woods and Glen Doherty, former Navy SEALs killed while defending the Benghazi consulate in Libya in 2012.

AMERICA'S MIGHTY WARRIORS

In 2008 Debbie Lee founded America's Mighty Warriors, a non-profit organization to honor, support, and encourage the troops and their families. It is dedicated to Marc Alan Lee's memory and his request in his last letter home, which reads: "So to all my family and friends, do me a favor and pass on the kindness, the love, the precious gift of human life to each other..."

She's opened Heroes Hope Home in Arizona where families of the fallen can stay for a week, all expenses paid. They can relax and ask hard questions like, "What do you do on birthdays? How do you celebrate that when they're gone? What do I do at Christmas? How do I do anything?" With her unique perspective as both a widow and the mother of a fallen SEAL, Debbie aids in their grieving and in the healing process.

Debbie Lee also hosts a Gold Star family camp on one thousand wooded acres in Hawkins, Texas. It's a place to have fun and grieve naturally, where healing conversations happen while horse-back riding, swimming, mountain biking, or at meals.

Lee's purpose is to be an encourager and to give people hope, whether it's in a one-on-one conversation or when she speaks to hundreds. People need help and hope in so many circumstances: the loss of a loved one, returning from deployment, divorce, a medical crisis, suicide.

"It's hard," she says. "You're struggling, but there is always hope. You can survive, and you can make it through. Drugs won't do it, alcohol won't do it, and sex won't do it. The only thing that will get you through is a relationship with Jesus Christ. I would have quit if not for my faith. I would have turned to drugs, alcohol, even suicide, the pain was so intense.

I knew Christ as my Savior, and I knew he didn't waste pain. He had walked me through death before. I knew my strength and my comfort came from him."

The Angel of Courage statue stands on Debbie's desk, arms raised in triumph. It reminds her of the courage God gives her to bear her loss, the boldness she needs for her mission to support the troops, and the strength of an over-comer that she passes on to those who have lost a loved one in combat.

"I have confidence," she says "not in my strength, but God's strength."

Notable Quotable

"I won't pretend it will be easy, but the way you
can make it is to let Christ be your strength."
– Debbie Lee

Points to Remember

- Be courageous.
- Transform your pain into something positive.
- Recognize and appreciate the sacrifices of our military troops and their families.
- Give others the gift of hope.
- Pass on kindness to others.

Take Action

1. After her son's death, Debbie Lee found courage to get through another day, boldness to step into public speaking, and determination to help our military in many ways. Where do you need courage in your life?
2. What pain can you transform into a positive?
3. How often do you honor and thank those who protect and serve our country?
4. In what ways can you offer encouragement, compassion and hope to others?
5. Think of ways you can do kind acts for others.

To Learn More about Debbie Lee, America's Mighty Warriors, and US Navy SEALs

Her non-profit website: www.americasmightywarriors.org
US Navy SEALs: www.sealswcc.com

CHAPTER 2

SECRET NUMBER TWO: ACCEPT YOUR LIMITATIONS

THE STORY OF BOB MORTIMER

The dark country road curved. Tom Mortimer jerked the steering wheel of the car hard to the right. Then he swung left. The car swerved across the rain-slick road, brakes squealing. It smashed into a power pole and then rolled down an embankment.

Tom stumbled from the car and called to his brother. "Bob! Bob! Are you cut or hurt? Are you bleeding?"[6]

"No, I'm OK," answered Bob. He crawled from the wreck. "How about you?"

In the early morning Washington-State gloom, they stared at the outline of their bent, twisted car and wondered how they had walked away unharmed. Still high from a night of partying, drinking, and smoking marijuana, they laughed and shook their heads.

"This will be a great story to tell at the mill on Monday!" Bob joked.

Bob clawed up the slope onto the road. With his left hand he grabbed what he thought was a fence so he could climb over it. Instead he touched a downed high voltage power line, and 12,500 volts of electricity slashed through his body, felling him like a tree. His knees exploded as they hit the road. He slumped forward onto live wires that continued to sizzle on his chest.

Tom stared at his brother's stiff, motionless body. Sickening smoke rose from it. *Bob's dead!* he thought. *Dead. At twenty-one.* He sank to the ground, covered his face with his hands, and sobbed.

Then he heard a moan. He rushed over to pull Bob off the wires. One wire still smoldered on Bob's neck, holding him captive. Tom grabbed the rubber sole of Bob's shoe to free him and to avoid being electrocuted. There was no jolt of electricity, but Bob was still stuck. Then Tom forgot about his fear and pulled on Bob's forehead. Finally Bob was off the wire. Again there was no jolt of electricity. Later Tom learned that a transformer had blown down the road so electricity was not surging through the lines.

"Help!" he cried out. "Somebody help!"

He turned Bob on his back. Tom's stomach lurched at the sight. Bob's left arm curled crisp from fingertip to elbow. Where Bob's knees used to be, Tom saw only holes, blood, and bone. The flash of electricity had even consumed Bob's shirt. Instinctively, Tom put his ear to Bob's chest and heard a faint heartbeat. However, Bob's chest still burned so hot, that it seared and scarred Tom's face. Even so, he attempted CPR, beating on Bob's chest.

"Bob, inhale!" his brother pleaded. "Exhale!"

Desperate, he turned toward the road and flagged down a car. "Please help!" he sobbed.

An ambulance arrived and rushed Bob to a hospital in Olympia, the state capital, but medical personnel were unable to deal with his extensive injuries. Helicopter blades churned the early morning air as Bob was airlifted to a trauma hospital in Seattle.

Bob Mortimer's encounter with high voltage electrical wires that night resulted in the amputation of his left arm and both legs.

"Sometimes you don't walk away," says Bob.

He lived without hope through a long, painful recovery until he realized his real recovery had nothing to do with his missing limbs; it had everything to do with accepting himself.

Bob Mortimer is now an evangelist and a motivational speaker and tells his audiences, "The only handicap you'll ever have is the one you put on yourself."

GROWING UP

One of seven children growing up on a farm in Ohio, Bob remembers his home as an uncomfortable place to live. His dad used prescription drugs and alcohol to dull his emotional pain, but that pain often exploded on the kids like a thunderstorm. Bob, being one of the youngest, watched as each of his older brothers joined the army just to get out of the house. He saw his dad struggle to make changes in his life, but the only change he made was their address. At sixteen, Bob moved with his family to South Dakota for a new start. His mom cleaned rooms at a motel, and his dad made excuses not to go to work. Bob took a hard look at his home life and thought, *Things aren't right; things aren't the way they should be.*

One morning he went to wake his dad up for work and found him dead from an overdose. Bob admits thinking, *Good. Now things will change!* I didn't cry for my father. I cried enough tears for him when he was alive. I didn't have any more tears when he died."

MANY MOVES

Bob, his younger sister, and his mother packed everything they owned into the back of their pickup truck and moved to Hoquiam, Washington, in the rainy Pacific Northwest.

Bob says now, "In Hoquiam, there are only two things you need to know. First, how to pronounce it [Ho-kwi-um] and second, that in the state of Washington it rains a lot, but in Hoquiam it rains a lot more!"

Bob walked down cold, rainy streets searching for acceptance, longing for someone to listen to him, and wanting to hear someone say "I love you." He didn't find that in healthy places, so he partied, drank and used drugs in an attempt to fill his need.

Looking back he says, "When you get on that road, it never spirals up, it only spirals down."

Soon Bob spun out of control. He dropped out of high school at seventeen. A few years later, when the partying, drinking and drugging got old, Bob decided he needed a change. He moved back to Ohio, flipping burgers for a living, but didn't change his drug-using behavior. In two years time he borrowed and stole money from his friends. When he had used up every favor possible, he once again thought, *I need to change.*

He remembered that there were good timber jobs back in Hoquiam and convinced his brother Tom, who had stayed in

Ohio, to join him. Timber was king in the 1970s, so they both found good-paying union jobs at the sawmill. It was "young man, hard spittin', swearin' kind of work," he says. But he didn't change his ways. "What was important in my life were the parties, the dope, and the beer."

THE ACCIDENT

On April 24, 1976, Bob slipped on his shoes for the last time and drove with Tom fifty miles to Olympia to see old friends. After midnight—many drinks and much dope later—they changed their plans and decided not to stay overnight in Olympia. Instead they drove home on back roads to avoid the highway patrol. In their impaired condition, they couldn't keep the car on those tricky, winding, rain-soaked roads. The choices they made that night still haunt them.

PAYING IN PAIN

Bob awakened in the Intensive Care Unit inside a web of tubes and wires. He was even chained to the bed so he wouldn't hurt himself. His mother and brother Tom sat nearby, their faces etched with sorrow. Filled with guilt, and blaming himself for the accident, Tom whispered, "I wish we could turn back the clock. I wish I could trade places with you."

Every inch of Bob's body throbbed. His mother tried in vain to find a place to touch him that wasn't painful. But gut-wrenching, mind-numbing pain wracked his body. Shattered bones, burned skin, useless limbs.

"Some nights will kick the man right out of you," remembers Bob.

A doctor appeared with a release form. "I'm sorry. We'll have to amputate your injured arm. Could you sign here?" he asked.

Without a second thought, Bob signed the form. He never wanted to see his crisp, gnarled, swollen left arm again.

Two weeks later the doctors amputated his right leg, and several months later they amputated his left leg. Bob spent six months in the hospital recovering from surgeries and the long, excruciating process of skin grafting.

"Things had changed, but all *this* change had brought me was pain," Bob recalls. "By the time they cut off my third limb, I thought I'd paid enough for my mistake. I paid in pain."

BEGINNING RECOVERY

Bob slowly adapted to life in a wheelchair, and he learned how to drive a car using hand controls and a prosthetic arm. His life had changed, but once again, Bob didn't change his behavior. He coped with his trauma and pain by using drugs and alcohol.

He says now, "Sometimes it's easier to go back than to change. It was easier to go back to things that messed me up, that wrecked my freedoms."

Bob felt as trapped and scared as a caged animal. Who would accept him with scars where there once was skin, with stumps where there once had been legs and an arm? As long as he had dope in his pocket, he found acceptance, but when his pockets were empty, he was alone.

During this troubled time, he met Darla, the babysitter for his sister's children. A strong friend, she helped him realize that his handicaps had nothing to do with his missing limbs. Bob admitted his problems to her and asked for help. Darla knew where he could get help and invited Bob to her church.

The Real Recovery

Bob rolled his wheelchair to the back row of the church. "This is far enough," he whispered to Darla.

Bob resisted listening to the pastor. *This is a joke. Who will accept me here?* he thought.

The pastor said unbelievable things like God loves and accepts us just as we are and that God would accept every scar, every loss, and every wrong road Bob had traveled. Bob fought the message, but the words sank deep into his heart. He longed for that love and acceptance to fill the emptiness inside him.

Then the pastor asked, "Is there anybody here who knows they need to be reconciled to the Father? Is there anyone who needs to be washed and cleansed by the blood of the Lamb, His Son, Jesus Christ?"

Bob wondered why the pastor spoke directly to him. *Why doesn't he just say "Bob"? I've run my life into the dirt. If God wants this life, he can have it. I'm not giving him much.*

Bob found the tug at his heart irresistible. For the first time he felt a deep need for a Savior. He wheeled to the front of the church. Weeping, he asked Christ to forgive his sins and come into his life.

"I became a whole man after the tears," remembers Bob. "I know I don't have legs, but what makes me whole was never in my shoes. I put Jesus Christ in my heart. I changed my life, and I changed my attitude."

Step by step, day by day, Bob followed Jesus. His desire to get drunk and stoned disappeared over time. The accident changed his body, but Jesus changed his soul. With Christ's help, Bob broke the chains of alcohol and drug abuse.

REAL CHANGE

Bob Mortimer began to make positive changes in his life. He married Darla, graduated from high school at age thirty, and earned a college degree in tax consulting. As he shared his story publically the first time, more and more speaking invitations poured in. Sometime later he returned to college to become a minister. Now as an evangelist, Bob's main ministry is speaking to people twenty-one and younger in schools, prisons, churches, and on military bases about how his faith in God gives him courage to overcome obstacles.

Sometimes Bob wonders how his life would be different if he still had his arm and legs. "Maybe I could get married…I did that! Maybe I could have children and raise a family…I did that! I have three children! Maybe I could have a job with purpose and meaning…I have that!" Despite his injuries, Bob has a complete life that God is using.

BIKING ACROSS AMERICA

In the summer of 2008, Bob Mortimer and his family bicycled across America sharing their message of hope in Christ and encouraging all of us to do something with that hope. They started in the state of Washington and ended at the Statue of Liberty on the seventh anniversary of 9/11, calling their trek Hope and Courage Across America. Bob rode a handcycle on the twenty-five-hundred-mile journey.

"It's not about the miles; it's about the message,"[7] says Bob. "The journey of Hope and Courage is all about pressing on. So is the journey of life."[8]

Back home in Gig Harbor, Washington, the Mortimers discovered they missed sharing their message at a slow pace while pedaling bicycles, so in 2011 they made a longer, six-month bicycle trip from Long Beach, California, to Florida—Hope and Courage across America, southern style.

In 2011 Bob Mortimer told his story in the *Hope and Courage Across America*. He wants people to recognize that we all have limitations, not only physical ones but also the limitation of behaviors like gambling and using drugs, alcohol, and pornography. Even our bad attitudes can limit us. When we let these things control our lives, they cripple and disable us. They keep us from being who God wants us to be. "Surrender these limitations to God," says Bob. "Ask him for courage to take a step forward, knowing that he will meet you."

Bob Mortimer was transformed when he surrendered all the broken pieces of his life to Jesus Christ. In Christ's power he found courage to overcome his drug and alcohol addictions, and the horrific injuries from the accident. In Christ's love, Bob found the ability to accept himself just the way he is. Even though people still stare and refer to him as "the man with no legs," he's given up the right to be offended. God helps him turn each negative comment into a positive experience.

His blue eyes sparkle as he says, "Accept the things that make you different from everybody else. When you can do that, it makes it so much easier for everyone else to accept you. I'm comfortable in my own skin; I'm OK with my body. This is just the way I look, but inside is who I am."

Notable Quotable

"Accept the things that make you different from everybody else. I'm comfortable in my own skin; I'm OK with my body. This is just the way I look, but inside is who I am."
– Bob Mortimer

Points to Remember

- Accept what makes you different from everybody else.
- Surrender your limitations to God.
- Give up your right to be offended.
- Be all that God wants you to be.
- Ask God for the courage to make positive changes in your life.

Take Action

1. Bob Mortimer has obvious physical differences from others because he's missing both legs and an arm. He learned to accept those differences when he accepted Christ's love for him. Have you accepted your differences?
2. We all have weaknesses and limitations. How often do you surrender those to God so he can use you?
3. When others say unkind things, do you fight back, fester with anger, or hold a grudge? What changes do you need to make to give up your right to be offended?
4. What attitudes and behaviors keep you from being all God wants you to be?
5. Life-change takes courage. Where do you find your courage?

To Learn More about Bob Mortimer

Hope and Courage Journey Across America: www.hcjour-
ney.org

His book: *Hope and Courage Across America.* ISBN 13:978-1-
46103220607 c2011.

CHAPTER 3

SECRET NUMBER THREE: SING THROUGH YOUR TROUBLES

THE STORY OF LISA ANN HAMMOND

L isa Ann took a deep breath and cradled the microphone in both hands. She closed her eyes and immersed herself in the prayerful words and soft melody of "Touch Through Me." As the sound track started to play, she sang.

Her clear, sparkling voice filled the church. The choir members stopped their practice to listen. The pastor stood speechless. A hush settled over everyone.

They didn't hear Lisa Ann's usual coughs or bursts of noise. They didn't see Lisa Ann's usual head jerks or face twitching. As she continued to sing, tears ran down the cheeks of some who listened.

The pastor at Roaring Fork Baptist Church in Gatlinburg, Tennessee, had been reluctant to let Lisa Ann sing, thinking her tics and shouts would get in the way. But now he asked her to sing at every service. Since the church was located in the tourist area of the Smoky Mountains, one Sunday visitor asked Lisa Ann if she traveled to other churches to sing.

"No, but I'd like to," she answered and gave him her contact information. A few days later, he called and asked her to sing at his church in South Carolina. Other invitations followed and today, Lisa Ann travels throughout the US and beyond, singing praise songs and sharing about God's work in her life.

Today she says, "I always loved to sing, but had no training. But now, I finally had a career, the first career of my life—that of a gospel singer. The Lord gave me a purpose in life, and he gave me a job!"[9]

Lisa Ann Hammond has Tourette Syndrome, a neurological disorder that causes involuntary movements and vocalizations. She is aware of her twitches and noises, although her control over the signals that her brain sends to her body is limited. There is no cure for Tourette's, only medication that sometimes helps minimize the symptoms.

Even today she struggles with commonplace tasks. When using a computer keyboard, she compulsively picks at the keys, so she uses a computer tablet instead. On the phone she pushes buttons and disconnects the call. Driving is difficult because of her head jerks. Sometimes she yells "Hey!" in a crowd, and everyone around her thinks she's calling them. She can't attend movies or any theater events due to her involuntary noises. She carefully chooses clothing without lace trim and beads because she might pull them off.

"It sounds like I'm crazy, but Tourette's is neurological, not psychiatric," she says.

She faces challenges and misunderstandings almost daily, but when she sings for God's glory, the Lord's comforting touch takes away her affliction.

The Beginning of Tourette's

When Lisa Ann was in kindergarten in Ohio, she licked her lips so often they became raw. All her school pictures show a red ring around her mouth. Looking back, she says her symptoms then were very mild and could be explained away as habits. However, over the next few years she started to blink her eyes uncontrollably, jerk her head, and touch things repetitively. Her face began to twitch, and she uttered sounds like *mmm, fa,* clearing her throat, hiccups, coughs, and even shrieks. Her symptoms came and went and changed over time.

"Lisa Ann, why do you do such weird things?" her friends asked. "Can't you stop making those noises?"

"I'm not doing it on purpose!" Lisa Ann replied.

Her mother took her to several doctors, but no one knew what was wrong. Unfortunately, not much was known about Tourette's in the 1970s and 1980s. In fact, the average time lapse between onset of symptoms and diagnosis is seven to ten years.

As Lisa Ann's jerks worsened and her utterances grew louder, friends shied away from her, several parents referred to her as mentally ill, and teachers secretly charted her unusual behaviors.

One teacher scolded her in front of the rest of the students. "Lisa Ann, if you would quit making those noises, you would do a lot better in class!"

All the students turned to look at Lisa Ann. Snickers and laughter erupted all over the classroom. She sank lower in her seat. Her face reddened, she twitched, and her noises didn't go away. In fact, her embarrassment made them worse.

REMOVED FROM SCHOOL

By the time Lisa Ann was twelve-years-old, her symptoms were at their worst. One day she was called into the junior high school counselor's office.

"We have to take you home," the counselor said, not offering any other explanation.

The counselor knocked on the Hammonds' front door. When Lisa Ann's mother, Lois, opened the door, her eyes widened to see her daughter with the school counselor.

"Mrs. Hammond, Lisa Ann can no longer attend school until we find out what is wrong with her. She's just too disruptive to others in class."

"What?" asked Lois. Her voice grew louder. "What did you just say?"

"We'll be in touch," the counselor said as she squared her shoulders and left.

Lisa Ann and her mother stood at the door in shocked silence. Lisa Ann felt helpless and confused. Her stomach was in knots.

"I felt that they thought I was crazy, but I knew I was normal, except I was doing strange things. I always knew what I was doing, but I couldn't stop," says Lisa Ann remembering that incident.

For the next two years, a school tutor taught Lisa Ann at home for only one hour a day. She felt completely isolated. Lisa Ann's friends were afraid to be around her because they didn't know what was wrong with her. She felt like a prisoner in her own body without any control over her jerks and shouts.

About that time, Public Law 94-142 was passed, allowing equal access to education for students with disabilities. Lois advocated for a full-time tutor, and Lisa Ann retained her own Ohio Legal Rights lawyer.

At long last, a doctor diagnosed Tourette Syndrome (TS). Both Lisa Ann and her mother felt some relief because they finally had a reason for Lisa Ann's behavior. However, their relief was short-lived when they learned there was no cure for TS, only prescription drugs that helped reduce the symptoms.

SUPPORT FOR LISA ANN

Lois Hammond was always Lisa Ann's biggest supporter. "She has been the one to stick by me my whole life," says Lisa Ann. Lois delved into medical literature for answers to her daughter's behavior, fought for her at school in unfair situations, and advocated for her with doctors. Few cases of TS were identified at the time, yet Lois started the Tourette Syndrome Association of Ohio and organized support groups throughout the state. Countless times, Lois defended her daughter and educated those around her about Tourette's.

Others showed love and support in special ways. Lisa Ann's father played softball with her and coached her girls' team. When her symptoms worsened, he took her on trips to a local state park. Another family friend, Dawn, stood by the Hammonds through all of Lisa Ann's turmoil. Dawn often took Lisa Ann to the Cincinnati Nature Center and showed understanding even when Lisa Ann screamed at the top of her lungs.

Drug Trials and Return to School

When Lisa Ann was fourteen, the prescribed drugs she was taking were not effectively reducing her symptoms. Her doctor recommended a new drug that was undergoing clinical trials. In order to try it, Lisa Ann had to quit taking all other drugs and tranquilizers. For two weeks she suffered excruciating withdrawal. Her parents removed most of the furniture from her bedroom because her arms and legs thrashed about violently. Her whole body shook, and exhaustion overtook her. She cried and screamed for help. Her mother and father held her tight and rubbed alcohol on her legs to ease the throbbing pain.

"It was like a nightmare, and I believe I have put most of it out of my mind, since I can only remember a little of that time," Lisa Ann recollects.

Once all drugs were out of her system, she started taking the new drug, Catapres, but her TS symptoms didn't improve right away. She visited the hospital three times a week for blood tests. One day her vocalizations were especially loud as she walked through the emergency room past a patient undergoing treatment. At that exact moment, a scream erupted from Lisa Ann. The startled patient sat upright, and the attending nurse dropped a bedpan that crashed to the floor.

"The incident was not funny at the time, but it is kind of funny now when I think of it!" says Lisa Ann.

After six weeks on Catapres, her symptoms greatly improved and she could return to school, which was now high school.

Lisa Ann remembers "I was really scared when I went back to school again. Everything was strange to me, even the way the school smelled. It was hard. After all, I had not been with anyone, except my family for two years."

College Years

Despite the missed years at school, Lisa Ann graduated from high school with her class. She interviewed and applied for several jobs, but no one hired her because of her Tourette's. At age eighteen, she applied for Supplemental Security Income (SSI) available to those who had never worked nor were expected to work in the future due to severe disabilities.

Lisa Ann said later, "I detested being on Social Security. It was so degrading to think that I had to have the government take care of me, and I vowed to go off it as soon as I could."

Lisa Ann continued her education at the University of Cincinnati and lived in a dormitory with other students. She thought she was enjoying the normal college student life, going to bars and searching for acceptance, but all the while she was searching for something more. Unfortunately, she built up a tolerance to Catapres, and her debilitating symptoms returned. She felt out of control, lost, and desperate for help. Her best friend invited her to church, where for the first time she heard about Jesus. She knew she needed him as a Savior, a helper, and a guide. That night she got down on her knees and asked Jesus to come into her heart and forgive her of her sins. Her life changed dramatically. The days looked brighter, and hope flooded her heart. She started attending church and reading the Bible. She quit drinking and going to bars, and she threw her rock music and short skirts into the dumpster outside her dormitory.

"The Bible tells us when we are saved we become a new creature, and truly that had happened to me. I wasn't the same person, and I no longer was searching. I found what I was looking for when I found out about Jesus and asked him to save me."

During that time, Lisa Ann discovered that when she sang, she had no Tourette symptoms. She frequented Kings Island in Cincinnati, an amusement park that had a recording studio. For about five dollars she sang a song or two and got a recording. When she listened to it, she heard her own steady voice, free of unwanted noises. Bolstered by that, she sang in her new church and even with a street ministry in Cincinnati's ghettos.

A New Career

After college, she looked for employment, but once again her symptoms made her unemployable. Discouragement and disappointment weighed her down.

"Little did I know that God had it all in His plan and was going to give me an exciting and unbelievable job singing for Him!" she said later.

Since she could not find a job in Ohio, she moved back with her parents in Tennessee. Sadly, she thought this might be the end of independent living for her.

Lisa Ann searched for a church family that would accept her disruptive symptoms. She found Roaring Fork Baptist Church where the pastor showed compassion for her condition. The church welcomed her, and she began to sing there on a regular basis.

As she received more invitations to sing, Lisa Ann traveled and earned an income from love offerings. She called her Social Security representative to stop the SSI payments, because Lisa Ann believed the Lord would provide for her.

The representative answered curtly, "You'll be sorry. You will never get on it again!"

Lisa Ann worried about her decision. "But then it became evident that God was going to provide for me, and I became elated that I was able to earn my own way!"

Soon after, Lisa Ann recorded her songs and started to receive even more income from the sales.

JOURNEY TO JAPAN

In 1997 Pilot International invited Lisa Ann Hammond to sing at their international convention in Washington, D.C. They raised funds for brain disorder research and requested popular secular songs. However, Lisa Ann did not want to compromise her decision to sing about her faith. She told several thousand members how God was using her through her Tourette's symptoms, and she sang three songs. When she finished, the audience fell silent. She thought they were upset with the religious content of her songs. Then suddenly all the audience members rose to their feet, applauding and shouting bravos.

A crowd stampeded to the table where Lisa Ann's recordings were for sale. When she quickly sold out and took orders, she felt like a rock star.

A few Japanese ladies at the convention asked if Lisa Ann would give a concert in Japan. She agreed, thinking nothing would come of it, but within weeks the trip was arranged.

Lisa Ann gave seven concerts in seven cities for the Pilot Club organization in Japan. She shared God's love for her listeners and ended each concert with a song she wrote, "In Heaven We'll Be Free." She tenderly expressed her longing for God's promise of a new body without Tourette's.

In heaven I'll be free from all my worries and my cares,
There'll be no more sickness, no more sadness, no more tears.
Most of all there'll be my Savior,
Who has been so kind, you see,
The One who cared so very much,
That he came and died for me. [10]

At her last concert during a question-and-answer time, a Japanese gentleman asked in perfect English, "How can you pray to your God and be so happy when he has given you Tourette Syndrome?"

Lisa Ann answered, "God is good, even in our weaknesses." She continued to tell him, and hundreds of others at the concert, how she had found her Jesus. Afterwards, she learned that man was quite influential as the emperor's interpreter.

"You Are the Song in Me"

Today, Lisa Ann Hammond's symptoms are still with her, and she often encounters unkindness and rude remarks. Recently, a boutique shopkeeper thought she was drunk and asked her to leave the store. Other times she overhears people saying, "She's weird!" She wishes others could look past her Tourette's and see her as a person.

"I want to tell them that I have a heart and feelings, but I just try to love them like Jesus would. Most days I'm good at loving them, but other days I fail miserably."

When she tells audiences how God changed her life, her tics and noises are on full display for all to see. She depends on God for the courage to stand in front of others, because her symptoms are worse when she's under the stress of public speaking. She overcomes her fear and symptoms by faith and inspires others to overcome their own obstacles with the same faith, courage, and positive attitude.

Lisa Ann Hammond has produced seven CDs of her songs and hopes to make another. "I'd like to keep singing for Jesus and go places I have never been," she says. "And I want to continue to tell others about how Jesus has changed my life and how He can change theirs if they would only let Him."

One song she wrote sums up her conviction to let her life sing through her troubles:

You are the song in me,
And that is why I sing...
Lord, this song I sing is true,
For I have made my choice
To always sing for You.[11]

Notable Quotable

"I have had a unique, challenging life, but I
give all the credit to God for being my
strength to overcome obstacles."
– Lisa Ann Hammond

Points to Remember

- Trust God's plan for your life.
- Praise God during the tough times.
- Depend on God to meet your needs.
- Do not compromise your convictions.
- Counter criticism with love.

Take Action

1. By God's grace, Lisa Ann Hammond became a gospel singer. She trusted God every step of the way. How much do you trust God's plan for your life?
2. How often do you praise God in song or prayer when the going gets rough?
3. Lisa Ann took a bold step in stopping her SSI payments. She knew that God would meet her needs. When have you depended on God to meet your needs?
4. When asked to sing secular songs, Lisa Ann politely refuses. She has made a commitment to sing for Jesus and doesn't want to compromise. In what area of your life can you stand firm upon your convictions?
5. How often do you counter criticism with a smile, a kind gesture, or forgiveness?

To Learn More about Lisa Ann Hammond and Tourette Syndrome

Her website: www.LisaAnnHammond.com

Her recordings: *His Comforting Touch, To God Be the Glory, Hymns from My Heart, You Are the Song in Me, Oh What a Day That Will Be, Lisa Ann's Greatest Hits #1, Praise His Name*

His Comforting Touch Music Ministry: for bookings call 843-503-4180

Tourette Syndrome Association: http://tsa-usa.org

CHAPTER 4

SECRET NUMBER FOUR: YOUR HISTORY IS PART OF YOUR DESTINY

THE STORY OF DR. HEJAL PATEL

"I'm sorry, we didn't get all the cancer," the surgeon announced to Hejal Patel and his parents. "You have two options. Either you live with the surgery we've done and take the risk of this cancer returning, or let us amputate your arm.[12]"

Thirteen-year old Hejal was recovering from an eleven-hour cancer surgery on his right arm. The surgeon's announcement left a heavy silence in the hospital room. Hejal and his parents stared wide-eyed at the doctor in disbelief.

Mr. Patel's trembling voice broke the stillness. "Can you take my arm and give it to my son?"

Within days, Hejal and his parents made the decision to amputate Hejal's right arm. He chose life, even though

41

it meant losing a limb. He recalls telling his parents, "We'll get through this; it's not the end of the world."

The night before the surgery, Hejal tossed and turned in bed. He heard his parents sobbing in the next room. Their outpouring of emotion embarrassed Hejal, but mostly he felt helpless because he could not ease their pain.

That was twenty years ago. Dr. Hejal Patel is now a radiation oncologist treating people with cancer. He went from cancer patient to cancer survivor to cancer doctor. Very early in his treatment, he looked at his surgeon, Dr. William Dunham, and said, "Doctor, get me well, get me strong again, because I want *your* job. I want to be a doctor and treat cancer."

He says now, "I was destined to be a doctor the day I was diagnosed!"

DISCOVERY OF CANCER

Hejal Patel grew up in Auburn, Alabama, the son of hard-working immigrant parents from India. One night while mopping floors at a grocery store, he felt a strange pain in his upper right arm. He wondered: *Did I pitch that ball too fast yesterday? Did I just sleep on my arm the wrong way?* But the pain persisted for weeks.

During school's Christmas break, his parents took him to a doctor. Hejal thought he might have a small fracture in his arm. If he got a cast, it would be a cool thing to show off at school. The doctor took an x-ray and did find a fracture in Hejal's arm, but he also found something else. He ordered more tests: a computed tomography (CT) scan, a magnetic resonance imaging (MRI), and a bone scan. The tests revealed a tumor growing inside the bone.

"I'm highly suspicious that this is cancer. You need to see a specialist in Birmingham," the doctor said.

Hejal was stunned. His parents shook their heads. "This can't be!" they exclaimed. "He's only thirteen!"

Nevertheless, they traveled to Birmingham, a three-hour drive from Auburn, to meet Dr. William Dunham, who specialized in bone cancer. He took a bone biopsy which Hejal admits "hurt like hell." The results confirmed it was indeed a malignancy—osteosarcoma[13], a rare bone cancer affecting teens.

HEJAL'S FIGHT

Hejal's treatment plan was to start chemotherapy, examine the tumor again, try to save the arm by removing the tumor, then follow up with more chemotherapy. Naturally curious with a quick mind, Hejal read about his cancer, knew all the terminology, and asked lots of questions.

Although Hejal remained optimistic, nothing prepared him for the miserable chemotherapy. Twenty years ago, anti-nausea medications didn't exist. Hejal's parents drove him to the Birmingham hospital every Thursday night where he stayed until Sunday evening. As the medicine dripped slowly into his bloodstream through an intravenous (IV) needle, he had a salty taste in his mouth, and sometimes a metallic taste. Both were nauseating.

He remembers, "I puked my guts out for ninety-six hours straight." He lost weight, fatigue drained him, and his hair fell out. "It was not an easy battle at all. It was a fight, it was a fight, it was a fight, it was a fight."

Yet Hejal refused to stay home and be depressed. Instead he strove to keep his mind occupied and graduate from high school on time. He went to school every day except on the Fridays he had treatments. His life narrowed down to just classes and cancer treatments. There was no time or energy for anything else. While other kids went to dances, movies, or Friday night football games, Hejal fought for his life, and did his homework.

After a month of chemo and the surgery on his arm to remove the tumor, Hejal received the bad news. He would lose his right arm. The news was especially grim because he was right-handed.

Making Adjustments

Traveling home in the car after his amputation, Hejal grabbed a yellow pad of paper and a pencil and tried to write with his left hand. "It was absolutely chicken scratch!" he remembers. Determined to write when he returned to school in the fall, he practiced writing a paragraph every day for three months until he could read his own writing.

He relearned keyboarding by centering his left hand on the keyboard. With lots of practice, he found he typed even faster than he believed was possible.

With the loss of his arm, Hejal learned to deal with another obstacle—phantom pain. His brain kept firing signals to an arm that no longer existed. He felt like his arm floated above his head and he couldn't bring it down, even though it tired him. He still feels it to this day, but he diverts his thoughts to something else. "Mental focus is the key," he says.

Returning to high school meant facing his teachers and classmates. Hejal had told some of them that he was sick, but few knew he had cancer. Now he couldn't hide from them the fact that he'd lost his arm. Reliving that moment he says, "I wanted to deal with this on my own, so I didn't want to tell anybody. There weren't a lot of people who would understand what I was going through. I didn't want to admit that I had cancer."

Fortunately, the teachers and kids at school *did* understand he'd been through a rough time, and his closest friends encouraged him. But even when they offered to help carry books or assist in other ways, Hejal didn't accept their help. "I was pretty stubborn when it came to that!"

DRIVER'S LICENSE

Like any sixteen-year-old teen, Hejal anticipated the freedom and independence that came with a driver's license. The State of Alabama required that he take disability training and qualify with a special instructor. Hejal drove several hours from his home to a special facility to meet with the driving instructor. One glance at all the extra accessories and devices in the car they wanted him to drive left Hejal astounded.

He turned to the instructor and pleaded, "Sir, let me just drive this car. Take off all of this junk and just let me drive. Just watch me!"

The instructor gave him the chance to drive for many miles and hours, going above and beyond an average driving test. Finally he said, "You know what? You're fine. You can drive without any restrictions on your license."

Reflecting on this incident, Dr. Patel says "I have tried to prove in my life that I am *not* disabled. I am faster and stronger than most people who have both arms!"

More Cancer

Just when Hejal thought cancer and treatments were behind him, a yearly scan showed a spot on his lung—another cancer. He hit a low point emotionally. He felt beaten down by his disease, his lack of energy, and the effects of years of chemotherapy. He had already lost fifty pounds on his slim frame. He endured another major surgery and more chemotherapy that involved more drugs for a much longer time. Through it all, his grit and determination fueled his fight.

"This was not going to get me down. I was not going to give up. If you give up, what are you going to do? In my mind there was no other option," Dr. Patel says now.

His high school victory came when he graduated with honors along with the rest of his class.

College

Hoping that college would be a new start, Hejal entered the University of Alabama premed program while still undergoing chemotherapy. Every day he wore the same black baseball cap to classes to conceal his hair loss. He scheduled classes so he wouldn't miss any and kept the weekends open for chemo instead of for fun, sports, or relaxation. Despite all this, he maintained a 4.0 GPA in his premed studies.

Finally, in his second year in college, Hejal's scans were negative, his hair grew back, and life returned to normal. He met his future wife, Stacy, in a college class. They became friends at the perfect time. She urged him to put some fun in his life.

"Don't work so hard," she told him. "You need to take a break once in a while!"

Dr. Patel admits, "She was what was missing; she made me whole again. I had the motivation and the drive because I was going to be a doctor come hell or high water. I was so focused on goals that I had forgotten to take time and enjoy myself."

With a burning desire to do cancer research, and on a fast track to becoming a doctor, Hejal approached his college professor who introduced him to Dr. Donald Miller, Deputy Director of the Tumor Institute at the university. Dr. Miller accepted Hejal as a research assistant. So in his second year as a biology major at college, but not yet a doctor or even a medical student, Hejal conducted "front line" cancer research.

Hejal graduated in three and a half years and was ranked as one of the top twenty college students in the country. He won so many awards in college that he can't recall them all. The most memorable was the *USA Today* All-USA College Academic First Team that gave him a trip to Washington, DC to receive the award. He used the award money to buy Stacy an engagement ring.

He married Stacy, studied another four years at the University of Alabama School of Medicine, and earned his medical degree.

A CANCER DOCTOR

Dr. Patel's goal was always to be an oncologist—a cancer doctor. He trained another four years as a resident at the University of Louisville in Kentucky. He chose radiation oncology because of the use of electrons, gamma rays, and X-rays to treat cancer. "It is one of the most technology-driven medical specialties out there," he says. Patient-care also appealed to him. Radiation doctors form special bonds with patients because they see them every day for six weeks. Patients become like family to them.

As a cancer survivor himself, Hejal Patel can identify with his patients. He knows what it's like to live with lingering complications, such as the probability of being sterile. His doctors had warned him about this due to his extensive chemotherapy. Nevertheless, while he was still a medical resident, he became a father. He says that the birth of his daughter was "quite fantastic!"

WORKING WITH PATIENTS

Working with cancer patients can be emotional: sometimes uplifting, and sometimes heartbreaking. The harsh reality is that some patients die. When Dr. Patel loses a patient, he cries. On the other hand, when a patient has a clear CT scan and the cancer is gone, he cheers. "Anybody who says they don't take their job home and they're in oncology is probably lying," he says.

Knowing that Dr. Patel battled cancer himself gives his patients hope that they, too, can survive. He is a great motivator to keep fighting. He tells them, "You want to go out fighting, fight tooth and nail. You want to stand for something. This will all be like a bad dream someday."

He uses humor to connect with each patient because it cuts the edge and helps them relax. One man told Dr. Patel about his love for southern biscuits and gravy. When the patient wasn't eating well, Dr. Patel joked, "Now, you can't be lying in this hospital bed. You've got to get up and cook me some biscuits and gravy!" It brought a smile to the man's face.

Another woman, bedridden with spinal cancer, expressed an interest in gardening. Dr. Patel invited her to his house when he mowed the lawn.

"Would you come over and pull some weeds?" he asked.

She returned the humor saying, "I'm coming. I know I didn't show up yesterday, but I'm coming over soon to pull your weeds!"

To young patients, Dr. Patel says "Consider this a big bump in the road. You're going to get past this. There is more road ahead of you. You can't give up. You're too young."

An Accomplished Life

Besides spending eleven-hour days with patients, Dr. Patel is also the President of the local Dothan, Alabama, chapter of the American Cancer Society, promoting cancer screenings and research. He and Stacy also volunteer every year at Camp Smile-A-Mile for children and teens with cancer. They give the kids a chance to forget about their illness, bald heads, and surgery scars, and just have fun swimming and fishing in Lake Martin and bunking in cabins. Those kids feel normal for a week or a weekend; they feel like kids again.

Now in his thirties, Dr. Hejal Patel has already lived an accomplished life. He devotes as much time as he can to the two children he has now because he wants them to be kids as long as possible. He remembers what it was like to be forced to deal with adult problems such as cancer and the possibility of dying at a young age. "I had to grow up so fast; I want my kids to stay kids," he says.

As a reminder of the six years of cancer surgeries and chemotherapy he's been through, he has kept his yellow writing pad and his black baseball cap. He never let go of his dream to be a doctor. He used mental focus and determination to push through the physical and emotional obstacles that came with the disease. If anyone knows cancer, Dr. Patel does. He's lived with it, survived it, studied it, researched it, treats thousands of people who have it, and hopes to find a cure for it.

"I've touched so many lives in what I do here. I've cured people of miserable cancer and got them out of a lot of pain. I'm a permanent part of people's lives. I go home happy that I've done so much."

Notable Quotable

"I was destined to be a doctor the day
I was diagnosed with cancer!"
– Dr. Hejal Patel

Points to Remember

- Fight your battles and don't give up.
- Pursue your dreams.
- Stay focused.
- Take time to enjoy life.
- Show compassion to others.

Take Action

1. What battles are you fighting right now? Dr. Patel fought cancer for six years. He used everything he could to overcome his disease—his mind, body, emotions, and spirit. How can you use his example to fight your own battles?
2. How much effort and planning do you put into pursuing your dreams? Think of one dream and one step you can take to achieve it.
3. To overcome the phantom pain of his amputated arm, Dr. Patel diverted his thoughts to something else. How can you use this powerful mental focus in your life?
4. Think of five ways you can enjoy your life more.
5. Life teaches us lessons. Where can you show compassion to others by using what you've learned and experienced in your own life?

TO LEARN MORE ABOUT DR. HEJAL C. PATEL AND CANCER

American Cancer Society: www.cancer.org
Camp Smile-A-Mile: www.campsam.org
21st Century Oncology: www.21stcenturyoncology.com

CHAPTER 5

SECRET NUMBER FIVE: FIND PEACE WITHIN YOUR PAIN

🙌

THE STORY OF PHYLLIS VAVOLD

As Phyllis Vavold and her husband, George, traveled west on Oregon's Highway 20 on July 11, 2004, they chatted while enjoying the drive to their vacation destination on the Oregon Coast. The top was down on their black Mustang convertible. The warm summer breeze whipped her hair and fanned her face. She drank in the tranquil high-desert scenery.

Suddenly, a stolen car racing east at 130 miles per hour slammed into them head-on. After a deafening crash, resulting in crushing weight, twisted metal, and shattered glass, pain gripped Phyllis, then darkness overcame her.

The other car, driven by a teenage boy joyriding with his friend, tumbled over the top of the Vavolds' Mustang, flipped three times, and exploded. Intense orange flames lit up the evening sky, and putrid black smoke strangled the air. The massive impact shoved the Vavolds' car into the middle of the highway.

Trapped and seriously injured, Phyllis drifted in and out of consciousness, remembering little of the accident. A Life Flight helicopter and crew circled for twenty minutes before they were able to land on the highway. The crew quickly cut through the mangled passenger door to extricate Phyllis. When she was lifted out, horrid pain seared through her body.

A short time later, as the helicopter approached St. Charles Medical Center in Bend, the pilot turned and told Phyllis, "We're just a couple of minutes from touchdown."[14]

Phyllis Vavold was the only survivor of that horrific car accident in which three people died, including her husband. In an instant, her life changed forever. The world she knew and loved ended. Left with severe injuries and the possibility of never walking again, she faced overwhelming challenges. Her physical recovery took over a year, but her emotional recovery from the trauma and loss of her husband took much longer.

She admits now, "It is a miracle that I survived... It is a miracle that I can walk... Another miracle of God is that I have peace of mind. He has brought me comfort and strength beyond anything I could have received from any other source."[15]

Phyllis Vavold is an author, inspirational speaker, and teacher of Bible studies she has written. She uses her own story of brokenness to bring hope to anyone who has a life-challenge too big to handle alone. She says, "God's bountiful grace is available in the calm days of life or in the midst of the raging storm of grief and pain."[16]

LIFE WITH GEORGE

Phyllis met George Vavold in Twin Falls, Idaho, while they were still in high school. They became inseparable sweethearts and married right after graduation. Eventually they had three children.

They moved to Nampa, Idaho, where George built their own four-bedroom home. George and Phyllis also established themselves in the community and in their church. Their love story lasted thirty-nine years, and Phyllis cherished everything about their life together: their faith in God, their marriage, their home, their children and their five grandchildren.

Without warning, the accident ripped away the life that she loved with George.

IN THE HOSPITAL

Still semiconscious, Phyllis was wheeled on a gurney into the emergency room. Doctors and nurses swarmed around her. One nurse scraped away pieces of glass from Phyllis' right hand. It felt like the nurse was scraping her hand raw.

"Where is George?" Phyllis murmured.

"You are the only one we are caring for right now," the nurse answered.

As the nurse cut away the shoe from her bloody right foot, Phyllis cried out in pain, "What has happened to my husband?"

"We're concentrating on *your* injuries," the nurse replied.

Unconsciousness returned. Soon Phyllis had X-rays revealing her extensive injuries: broken right hip, dislocated left hip, shattered right foot, broken ribs, fractured spine, knee trauma, multiple cuts and abrasions all over her body, and a concussion. The hospital listed her in grave condition. In the midst of the chaos, a doctor informed her that she needed emergency surgery on her hip that night.

The next day Phyllis awakened, still groggy from anesthesia. A tall, slender man with kind, gentle eyes stood over her. Chaplain Ray from St. Charles Medical Center spoke softly to her, explaining the car accident and her injuries. When Phyllis asked about her husband, the chaplain hesitated.

"He's gone, isn't he?" she asked.

He nodded and replied, "Yes."

Even before she asked, Phyllis suspected that George had not survived the head-on collision, but she struggled to accept it. She cried out, "I don't want to be a widow!" Then, exhausted, she drifted off to sleep.

Phyllis discovered later that her family had gathered in her hospital room and had witnessed her anguished outcry.

During her twelve days in the hospital, Phyllis had two more surgeries: one to place a filter in her abdomen for blood clots and another to reconstruct her shattered foot. She came to think of the operating room as her second home. She recalls that those days were "like the worst nightmare you can imagine," because of the unrelenting pain and heavy sedation. But Phyllis admits now that God prearranged the best care possible for her, since St. Charles Medical Center ranks high in orthopedic and trauma care.

RECOVERY AT CHERYL'S HOUSE

The Vavold family had many discussions about Phyllis' future care. Her daughter, Cheryl, felt impressed by the Lord to take Phyllis home with her. Cheryl knew it would be difficult with two children ages six and three, a two-week-old infant, and a husband, Kris, who attended college classes at night. Despite all this, Cheryl and Kris opened their home to Phyllis, arranged for a hospital bed and other equipment that Phyllis needed, and prepared the first-floor large bedroom for her.

"This room became my refuge in the midst of the tsunami of my life," says Phyllis. She was bedridden for four months, not allowed to dress herself, shower, or get up without help. Phyllis learned to accept care from Cheryl, but found it difficult to be so helpless and dependent, especially since she no longer had George.

Unable to read at first due to her concussion, Phyllis asked friends to read to her. She also listened to music. Cheryl prayed with her during the day and at night when Cheryl's infant awakened.

At times the medication wore off and allowed sharp edges of pain to close in on Phyllis. Then she listened to the soothing words of Scripture on a CD, and it calmed her every time. "I found that God's Word is powerful, comforting, and sustaining in the darkest moments of life," she recalls.

DIFFICULT DAYS

Sometime later, Phyllis faced unbearable lows. Not only did she need another surgery, but she also began to settle medical bills and insurance. In addition, she received a letter from one of the deceased boy's parents threatening to sue her for the car accident. Problems piled up. Her life was like a roller coaster plummeting downwards. She wept, even wailed, but she testifies now that "finding peace within the storm is God's specialty."[17] The lawsuit was dropped when the police report made it obvious that the Vavolds were not at fault for the accident.

Sometimes, when Phyllis's three-year-old granddaughter heard her weeping, the child would tiptoe to her bedside, stroke her arm, and tenderly say, "Don't cry, Grandma." Phyllis learned to guard her times of crying because of the effect it had on her grandchildren.

Weeks after arriving at Cheryl's house, Phyllis called Mona Dahlquist, a counselor who had been a widow, to invite Mona to visit. When Mona entered the room, Phyllis requested that she close the door.

"I have a question for you. It is deeply troubling me, and I have not shared it with anyone," Phyllis said.

"What is it?" asked Mona.

Phyllis whispered, "Is there a future for me?"

Mona sighed and said, "I can promise you God has a future planned just for you filled with hope and healing."

Mona reassured Phyllis that God promised to do *new* things in her life. She read Isaiah 42:9 (NIV) aloud: "See, the former things have taken place, and new things I declare."

God began preparing Phyllis for a new beginning. Mona visited Phyllis every week, counseled her, prayed with her, and gave her encouraging Scripture. Phyllis had to make the choice whether or not to trust in God's Word. "My only hope was to lean heavily on my God... Leaning means we put our faith in God's wisdom even when we cannot understand."[18]

Lying in her bed for endless hours, Phyllis faced another choice, "to wallow in my pain or to do something productive with my plight." She chose to read God's Word and to journal. When she wrote, God gave her spiritual insights that she used later in her book.

THE REHABILITATION CENTER

Four months after the accident, Phyllis needed physical therapy to strengthen her atrophied muscles. Her insurance paid only for inpatient therapy at the Elks Rehabilitation Hospital in Boise, thirty miles from Nampa. Phyllis had been surrounded by family and friends ever since the accident. Now, for the first time, she was alone and uprooted from her place of refuge.

Unnerved, she arrived at the hospital dreading more doctors and another hospital to get used to. To make matters worse, she shared a room with a woman who complained loudly all night. Finally, Phyllis was moved to a large private room with a view of beautiful autumn colors and the illuminated cross on Boise's foothills. As a nurse wheeled her down the hallway, Phyllis commented that she felt like a queen.

"Why don't you practice the queen wave?" the nurse suggested.

So Phyllis did. She lifted her arm in a regal wave all the way down the hall as she passed patients and staff.

Although fearful of being alone, Phyllis discovered that solitary time provided her with healing. She was alone with God in a way she had never experienced before. Everything in her life had been stripped away—her daily routines, independence, health, husband, home. "When I had nothing left but God, He was enough!" she said later. "Somewhere along my journey there came a time when I chose to allow God to take over completely."[19]

One day her doctor told her that the trauma of her accident alone had been enough to destroy her, but the loss of her husband added more than should have been tolerable. Looking back she says, "Once again God proved that He will strengthen the weakest, sustain the shakiest, and bring comfort to the tormented."

During her two-week stay at the rehabilitation facility, Phyllis grew stronger and began to walk with the help of a walker.

DEALING WITH GRIEF

With the support of her family, Phyllis celebrated her first Thanksgiving, Christmas, and Easter without George. On May 29, 2005, ten months after the accident, her son drove her to the tranquil green lawns of the cemetery where George was buried. It would have been Phyllis and George's fortieth wedding anniversary. Standing over George's grave, Phyllis and her son, George Jr., talked and cried together. All of a sudden, Phyllis felt an intense pain in her chest—not physical pain, but the pain of extreme heartache. At that moment, she realized that God had shielded her during the previous year from the agony of loss. Her broken body had needed time to heal. Now it was time to heal her broken heart. She later read in Psalm 23:4 (NIV): "Even though I walk *through* the valley of the shadow of death, I will fear no evil for you are with me."

"One cannot get over grief," Phyllis reflected. "One cannot ignore grief. The only way to get to the other side is *through* it."

"Did I ever complain? Yes! Did I ask why? Yes! Did I cry, even wail? Yes, yes, yes! Still I had a choice to focus on my pain and loss or focus on God and the provision He had for me."

In retrospect, Phyllis knows that the accident interrupted her love story with George, but her love relationship with God will never be interrupted. "There is no tragedy, no circumstance, and no force in heaven or on earth that can come between you and God, when you place your life in His hands."[20]

A New Beginning

The first time Phyllis was physically able to return to the home that she had shared with George for twenty-five years, memories overwhelmed her. Months had passed, and the house stood silent and empty. It no longer felt like home, because George wasn't there.

For many reasons, Phyllis made the difficult decision to sell the house: it was on acreage which Phyllis could not maintain by herself; it had stairs which challenged her; and it was out of town, far from family, church, and doctors. The process of preparing the house for sale lasted for months. Phyllis watched as others sorted and packed her possessions. She couldn't do anything except give orders. Her helpers held up every item and asked Phyllis, "Keep? donate? or trash?

Starting over was not easy. However, Phyllis pressed on and decided that a custom-built one-level home with extra-wide doors and halls would meet her needs. It was set in a private and secure area.

By the time she moved in, Phyllis was walking with a cane and finally driving her car again. The first night in her new home, she sat on the couch and watched the DVD of George's memorial. She thought, *This is familiar. George is familiar, and my life with him is familiar.* These thoughts gave her comfort in her new surroundings.

She decorated her bedroom in her favorite colors of lavender and cream, and in the great room, she displayed ten of the costumed porcelain dolls she had created.

A friend visiting her new home commented, "This house is so *you*, Phyllis."

Phyllis answered "I know! God built it for me!"[21]

SHARING HER STORY

From the onset of the accident, Phyllis Vavold wanted to share with her church family how God helped her through the long process of healing. Three months after the collision, she was wheeled onto the platform at church to give her testimony of God's grace. From time to time, she continued to tell and show her church family how God brought a miracle triumph out of tragedy.

A few years later, several people encouraged her to tell her story. Since then, Phyllis has had many opportunities to speak at women's events, women's retreats, and in churches all over the Northwest and in Arizona, California, and Tennessee.

She's also been on a worldwide radio broadcast through the program *Words to Live By,* and she taped a few episodes for a local Christian TV program. She felt compelled to write her story and publish it in 2010 as *Grace for the Raging Storm: A Story of God's Provision in the Midst of Tragedy and Loss.*

At the urging of a Bible study leader, Phyllis wrote *Covenant of Grace* in 2014, designed as a companion workbook to enhance the truths of *Grace for the Raging Storm.* Several churches have used the study, and Phyllis has taught it as well. That same year she also published another Bible study, *Recipe for Perseverance.* "Perseverance is the motto that I live by right now," she says. Always a student of Scripture, Phyllis feels God moved her into a new role of Bible teacher with her books.

Phyllis Vavold is still slightly limited in her mobility. She avoids stairs and getting down on the floor. She also had more surgery on her foot and her hip, but people around her see no evidence of the horrible trauma she's been through. She is a victim who, by God's grace, became a victor. She clung to God's promise of provision in Hebrews 4:16 (NIV). "Let us approach God's throne of grace with confidence, so that we may receive mercy and find grace to help us in our time of need." Now her heart's cry is for God to use her pain and bring blessing out of her tragedy.

Phyllis says, "I am an ordinary woman with an extraordinary story. In sharing my story, God has brought me healing in ways I could not have imagined. Although one season of my life has passed, another can now begin."[22]

Notable Quotable

"When I had nothing left but God, He was enough!"
– Phyllis Vavold

Points to Remember

- Find peace within your pain.
- Lean on God even when you don't understand the whys of your circumstance.
- Face your fears.
- God can shield you from pain until you are able to handle it.
- Study God's Word to prepare and strengthen you for future troubles.

Take Action

1. Phyllis Vavold found that God's peace was with her during her pain and personal storm. Where do you find peace within your pain?
2. Through her tremendous physical pain and loss, Phyllis leaned on God and his Word. How much faith do you have in God's wisdom when you don't understand your circumstances?
3. Phyllis faced her fears of being alone and making many life changes. What fears are you willing to face in your own life?

4. When has God shielded you from pain that you could not bear at the time?
5. How much time are you willing to spend studying God's Word in preparation for struggles you'll face in the future?

To Learn More about Phyllis Vavold

Her website: www.phyllisvavold.com

Her books:

Grace for the Raging Storm: A Story of God's Provision in the Midst of Tragedy and Loss, 2nd ed. (Nampa, ID: Phyllis Vavold Ministries, 2013).

Covenant of Grace – New Edition: A Companion Bible Study Workbook Designed to Enhance the Truths in Grace for the Raging Storm (Nampa, ID: Phyllis Vavold Ministries, 2014).

Recipe for Perseverance: Bible Study Workbook 1 Samuel 1–3 (Nampa, ID: Phyllis Vavold Ministries, 2014).

CHAPTER 6

SECRET NUMBER SIX: YOU'RE WORTH BEING HEALTHY

THE STORY OF BERNIE SALAZAR

"Bernie, why are you here? You're healthy enough and strong enough at this point to scale a fence and start running. So why are you still here?"[23]

Bernie Salazar stared at himself in the bathroom mirror. It was Week 10 of *The Biggest Loser* reality TV show, and he was one of ten remaining contestants. He had already lost eighty-eight pounds. Every muscle in his body screamed from the intense workouts. Exhaustion drained him. Escape seemed like a good option. He hid in the bathroom, the only place free from probing cameras. What had motivated him in the past failed to light a fire under him now. In his mind, Bernie mulled over the reasons for continuing on the show. He didn't want to disappoint anyone: his trainers, his friend Mike who hadn't made the cut for the show, all the people he had met in line during the casting calls, his mother, his brother, and his many friends who were cheering him on to victory. But where was he on the list?

Aloud he told his reflection in the mirror, "Bernie, you're here because you're worth seeing this through and living the life you've always wanted. You're worth being healthy."

Bernie said it, and he meant it. The reason he endured the long workouts and the strict diet of eighteen hundred to two thousand calories a day was for himself, not for anyone else. At that moment he realized that overcoming obesity wasn't going to be a quick fix or a temporary solution. It would be a journey, a lifelong commitment to healthy living.

"We can get far with our eyes closed," Bernie says today. "The hardest thing on the show was really looking at *me*."

During Season 5 of *The Biggest Loser* in 2008, Bernie Salazar shed one hundred and thirty pounds—almost 46 percent of his body weight—and went from 283 pounds to 153 pounds. Now a children's book author with a master's degree in education, Bernie dedicates his life to helping others lead a healthy lifestyle. As a motivational speaker, his desire is to help all people, especially those struggling with obesity, to completely regain control of their lives as he did.

BERNIE'S CHILDHOOD

Bernie was raised by a hardworking single mother. As a neonatal intensive-care nurse, his mother worked long hours, so Bernie and his younger brother were often left with their Mexican and Puerto Rican relatives, who fed them well.

When one of them made tacos, along with beans and rice, Bernie exclaimed "Oh my goodness! This is my favorite!"

When another offered him barbecued steak, Bernie said "Oh my goodness! *This* is my favorite!"

His enthusiastic appreciation made the relatives enjoy feeding him, and Bernie found he could get more food.

Although both Bernie and his brother played sports, Bernie's overeating caused him to add on pounds. He understands now that even as a child he used the comfort of accessible food as a coping mechanism. With the lack of a father figure in his life, and as the eldest son, he shouldered the responsibility to be a good kid and a positive role model for his younger brother. Food became his way of escaping from those self-imposed pressures.

Growing up in Northwest Indiana near Chicago, Bernie learned to treat everyone with respect. Social and outgoing, he got along with many people. He remembers hearing occasional comments about his weight, but fortunately, no one shunned him or excluded him.

High School and College

Bernie's weight first caused some problems in high school. At 195 pounds and five feet, five inches tall, he became self-conscious. He avoided swimming in PE classes because he had to take off his shirt. He made sure he was on the "shirts" team when they played "shirts" vs. "skins" (those wearing shirts vs. those without shirts). He knew who to hang out with, who to talk to, and who to avoid. His "strategic social maneuvering" worked well. Popular, with an upbeat personality and a contagious laugh, Bernie played baseball throughout high school, held student council positions, and was voted 1998 Prom King at George Rogers Clark High School in Hammond, Indiana.

While in high school he dated someone special who opened his eyes to his self-image. He learned the importance of being a quality individual on the inside and not judging himself or others on outward appearance alone.

Bernie continued his education at the University of Evansville in Indiana as an elementary education major. Always involved in life around him, he served as student government vice president, resident assistant, and rush chair for his fraternity, Sigma Phi Epsilon. Food still dominated his life, so he volunteered on a food advisory board to comment on the cafeteria food. Bernie said later, "I've never said no to an opportunity. It's not fair to say I don't like something unless I've tried it."

MOVING TO CHICAGO

Because he loved Chicago, Bernie moved there after graduating from college. One day, too late for a job interview because he got lost, he wandered into Lincoln Park Zoo, a place he considers "magical." Dressed in a suit and carrying his resume, he bumped into a zookeeper.

"Hey, this is a great place," he said. "How would I go about getting a job here?"

The zookeeper pointed him to the administration building.

Inside, the office manager asked, "What kind of job are you looking for?"

"I'm a teacher," Bernie replied. "I have my degree. I can show it to you. I just got it."

She sent him to the Zoo Education Department, and he discovered they were indeed looking for an educator.

They hired Bernie a week later with Project Noah (No One Aspires Higher), a literacy outreach program for kids.

Once a year as part of the program, a Chicago Bulls basketball player would read a story to the kids. While setting up for this event at the Bulls site, Bernie noticed an announcement for tryouts. The Chicago Bulls Matadors, "a fat guy dance team," needed dancers. Bernie's friends and coworkers encouraged him to try out. At the audition, Bernie was one of sixty-eight men vying for six places, and he was selected.

"It wasn't as much of a joke as I thought," recalls Bernie. The Matadors didn't just jiggle and wiggle for the crowd; they practiced a well-planned choreography. Bernie wore wacky clothes with knee socks and sprayed his hair red (the Bulls color) before he danced at sixteen home games. Being the tiniest dancer at almost three hundred pounds, Bernie topped a wobbly pyramid at half-time performances.

THE "BERNIE" CUPCAKE

When his zoo job lost funding, Bernie pursued a master's degree in education at the University of Illinois at Chicago. Also Spanish-speaking, he received an assistantship[24] teaching English as a Second Language (ESL) to Hispanic parents in the Little Village community. For eighteen months, his life was a blur, teaching during the day and taking classes at night. Much to his delight, a new bakery, Sensational Bites, opened in his neighborhood. Whenever Bernie had a bad day—or a good day or just a day—he visited the bakery. He fell in love with their mouthwatering Boston Crème Pie cupcake: angel food cake with creamy custard inside, dipped in a chocolate ganache.

Bernie asked the owner, "When are you going to name this after me so I can just ask for a 'Bernie'"?

Over time he consumed at least one hundred cupcakes, and the owner did rename the cupcake. Later on a *The Biggest Loser* episode, Bernie visited the bakery. When the episode aired, people all over the country were ordering the "Bernie" cupcake.

CASTING CALL

One morning during his time in Chicago, Bernie ate his usual pop-tart-and-soda breakfast and watched the news. He saw a casting call for *The Biggest Loser* and he thought, *I really have nothing to lose except the weight.* By now at his heaviest weight, he suffered from high blood pressure, sleep apnea, and acid reflux at night that "felt like someone poured hot Drano down my throat." Busy with graduate school and teaching English, he found no time to exercise. More pounds piled on, and Bernie grew tired of tight clothes and a permanent indentation from his waistband.

The Biggest Loser, Season 5 advertised for couples or teams of two, so Bernie convinced another Matador dancer, Mike, to join him at the casting call just for the fun of it.

He remembers saying, "We have a great backstory. We're the fat-guy dancers from the fattest city in the fattest country in the world. If we don't make the show, we can claim to be the biggest losers because we couldn't even make the show! If it's not a good time, it'll be a good story!"

In Chicago alone, five hundred people showed up for *The Biggest Loser* audition. In line, Bernie met women who couldn't have children due to their obesity, and some who used food to fill the loss of loved ones who had died. Many saw a place on the show as a chance to save their lives. These heart-wrenching stories sobered Bernie, and he vowed if he got on the show that he would use the opportunity to help others. Both Bernie and Mike passed several auditions and physical and psychological screenings, filled out lots of paperwork, and were flown to Los Angeles for even more auditions.

Bernie and Mike were upbeat about their obesity. Bernie explains, "We didn't go around every day thinking we were obese. We found a way to make it fun. We were Matadors! We knew what it was like to live life large; we just wanted to know if living life small was as much fun."

In the end, *The Biggest Loser* selected Bernie and sent Mike home. Before Mike left, he told Bernie, "I'm excited for you. You'd better win this thing!"

THE BIGGEST LOSER: COUPLES, SEASON 5

The 2008 show teamed Bernie with Brittany Aberle, a total stranger. Out of two hundred thousand people who tried out, only twenty made the show. Bernie admits now that he didn't know what he was getting into—the long hours of fitness training, aches, pains, and fatigue. He didn't realize he had more than a weight issue. He also had a lot of pent-up emotions to resolve.

The first three days proved brutal for him. He vomited food and liquids everywhere. His body resisted the intense level of activity. The medical team immediately pulled him from the show and sent him to the hospital. Frustrated but determined, Bernie thought, *I didn't come out here to lie in a bed.*

Soon Bernie was back in the show's routine. On a typical day he walked an hour on the treadmill, ate a snack, and spent forty-five minutes with his trainer lifting weights, doing sit-ups and pull-ups, then more time on a stair-step machine or doing other aerobic exercises. Throughout the day, he exercised five to seven hours. His heart pounded in his chest, he dripped with sweat, showered a lot, and changed his tee-shirt two to four times every day. He wore out a pair of athletic shoes every few weeks. When he developed blisters on his feet, a trainer popped them, taped them up, and sent him back to his workout.

Bernie survived ten weeks on the fifteen-week show before being voted off. Fortunately, by that time he had developed the inner and outer strength to continue his weight-loss journey at home. In the past he had blamed his failures on his weight and not on himself, but now he took responsibility for his eating behaviors.

Back in Chicago with two and a half months until the finale, Bernie hired a personal trainer, exercised two to three hours per day, ate well by choosing organic foods, and continued his newfound self-reflection. He ate eighteen hundred to twenty-one hundred calories a day while maintaining his dignity and his health. He says, "You can't live in extremes because it's not maintainable. Be consistent." He let go of his fast-food eating habits and parted ways with some of his friends who reinforced those habits. Bernie lost another forty-two pounds at home.

At the finale, Bernie won the "at home" biggest-loser award of one hundred thousand dollars. He beat out his closest competitor by one pound.

Looking back, Bernie says *The Biggest Loser* show helped him lose weight, but he gained so much more than he lost. "I gained inner confidence, motivation, a true belief in myself, a new relationship with my mother and brother, a good friend in Brittany, *and* the woman who was to become my life partner."

Marathons and Marriage

Bernie and Brittany continued their close friendship after the show. They ran the Rose Bowl Half Marathon (13.1 miles) together in 2009. Bernie reconnected with Brittany's cousin, Jennifer, whom he had met originally at *The Biggest Loser* tryouts and had seen again at the finale. Love drew them together, and they married in August 2010.

Bernie set another goal to run a full marathon (26.2 miles). He trained with a coach who taught him to focus on each step of the journey, not on the finish line or the completion time. So far he has completed three full marathons.

His Journey

Bernie Salazar has kept off the weight by exercising one and a half hours a day, five days per week. He changed his attitude about food and now sees it as fuel for his body. He adds more fruits and vegetables to his diet and limits his calories to roughly two thousand per day.

Since the show, Bernie founded Monstercise, LLC, for children's health and wellness and is a motivational speaker. His children's book, *Monstercise,* is forthcoming. He also works with several charities: Louie's Kids to help overcome obesity, Halo of Hope to combat chronic diseases, and the American Heart Association, which awarded him "The Power Award" in 2011 for his work as an ambassador to end strokes.

With determination and a positive attitude, Bernie took control of his life and his health. He pushed through the discomfort to achieve his weight loss. He embraced adversity so he could overcome it. The results, and his newfound confidence, made the effort worthwhile

Bernie Salazar's weight-loss journey opened new opportunities for him. Never one to say no to an experience, Bernie accepts new challenges. He says, "A true journey never has an end. Make sure you're leaving your marks along the way. Remember, you can stop and regroup, you can backtrack, but every day have the courage to start again. You can't be stopped if you keep on moving."

Notable Quotable

"You're worth seeing this through and living the life you've always wanted. You're worth being healthy."
– Bernie Salazar

Points to Remember

- Be healthy.
- Say yes to new opportunities.
- Learn from every experience.
- Judge others by their inner character, not their outer appearance.
- Be proud of your success.

Take Action

1. Bernie Salazar overcame his obesity by taking steps to achieve a healthy lifestyle. He changed his eating habits and added exercise and positive thinking. List changes you need to make to be healthy.
2. How open are you to new opportunities in your life?
3. How can you evaluate your experiences to learn from them?
4. What changes in your attitude will help you judge others by their inner character?
5. Do you ignore or downplay your successes? What can you do to celebrate them?

To Learn More about Bernie Salazar

His healthy family programming and children's book: *Monstercise*, available at www.mymonstercise.com

His motivational speaking: contact Bernie at biggestloser-bernie@gmail.com

CHAPTER 7

SECRET NUMBER SEVEN: NO ONE IS BEYOND HOPE

THE STORY OF STACY CLEVELAND

"I give up, Stacy! I'm going to recommend that you go to jail."[25]

The caseworker at Stacy's front door delivered the ultimatum. Stacy crossed her arms and glared at her.

I'll show you! she thought. *There is* no way *I'm going to jail. What would happen to my girls if I did?*

For days Stacy mulled over her options. Finally, her stubbornness melted into resolve, and she followed the recommendations to avoid jail: stop living with her drug-dealer boyfriend, stop using drugs, and start drug-abuse treatment.

At age twenty-nine, Stacy Cleveland found herself homeless, addicted to methamphetamine, and a single mom with two small children. She had lost her job and her housing and faced criminal charges for stealing money.

She says now, "I was numbing myself with drugs. I didn't see how bad my life was because I was numb to it. It all happened very quickly. I hit bottom."

After she started drug-abuse treatment, one final recommendation rescued her life. Her chemical-dependence counselor told her to move into a shelter. Stacy made only one phone call and found an opening at Seattle's Union Gospel Mission (UGM) Women and Children's Shelter. Now, sixteen years later, she is the director of that same shelter, overseeing twenty-five staff members and one hundred fifty women and children who live there at any given time.

EXPERIMENTING WITH DRUGS AND ALCOHOL

Although Stacy was born in Seattle, Washington, her family moved several times, and she lived in a succession of states as she grew up. Always the new kid on the block, she struggled to fit in and find acceptance with her peers. In middle school she dabbled with drugs and alcohol. "When you start using, there are ways in which it works for you," she says. The drugs helped her relax, especially in social situations. The partying group of kids readily accepted her because she shared their interests—drugs and alcohol.

Raised in a middleclass Christian home, Stacy didn't understand the pitfalls of addiction. Looking back she says, "I didn't have a picture of where addiction can take people because I didn't see it in my home life."

HER TWENTIES

She returned to Seattle to attend Seattle Pacific University. It felt like home to her, but her alcohol and drug use escalated. She met a boy, got pregnant, married him, and dropped out of college. After the birth of their daughter, Stacy's husband introduced her to cocaine. She got hooked and was quickly addicted. The marriage soon fell apart due to addiction, as well as her husband's neglect and abuse.

With a baby to support on her own, Stacy pulled herself together, quit using drugs, and went back to college with a major in biology and a minor in accounting. After she graduated, she worked at a bank and made a life for herself and her child. But without stable friends to support her, she allowed the old patterns to return. She said later, "I quickly went down the wrong path . . . downhill in every way."

Stacy moved in with a new boyfriend, a drug dealer with a criminal past. She used methamphetamine, hung out with a whole new crowd, and flirted with crime. By this time she had another baby, a beautiful, dark-haired daughter, but the spiral of her life continued downward. Stacy was evicted, and then her boyfriend went to jail. She stayed in several unsafe places; some even without running water. Day and night, a steady parade of drug users came and went. Stacy and her girls slept on couches or mattresses on the floor. Many times she worried that they would end up sleeping in a car.

At one temporary house, Stacy sat surrounded by boxes of her belongings. She glanced out the window, pondering her life. Delicate pink cherry blossoms fluttered in the May breeze. Their fragile beauty captivated her.

There is a beautiful life out there somewhere, she thought. *I want something better for my children. I want them to have that beauty in their lives.*

After two years on meth, Stacy longed for a different life, but what jolted her to change was the caseworker's visit with the very real threat of jail time.

SEATTLE'S UNION GOSPEL MISSION

In 1999, when Stacy Cleveland opened the heavy wooden doors of Seattle's UGM in the International District, she sensed she belonged there. "God knew I needed to get in quickly, and he opened that door."

Clutching her seven-year-old daughter's hand and cradling her five-month-old baby, she approached the front desk. An intern recognized her from Seattle Pacific University.

"Hi!" the intern greeted her. "Are you here to volunteer?"

Stacy hesitated. "No," she replied. "I'm checking in."

"Oh, are you volunteering to work with the kids?" the intern asked.

Stacy flushed with shame. "No we're here to stay. We're going to be living here."

Stacy bared her soul to the counselors at UGM. She wore her shame like a tacky, tattered blanket. Addiction and homelessness had never been a part of her family history. She wondered how her life had spun out of control. The counselors listened; nothing shocked them.

What a mess, Stacy thought. *I need to fix this. I need to take responsibility and find support around me.*

Stacy and her girls settled into Room 210. Coming off meth, Stacy moved in slow motion through a mental fog. Things happening around her didn't seem real. The rush of energy from meth vanished, leaving her exhausted. She just wanted to sleep. On top of the withdrawal symptoms, she discovered she was pregnant again. Fortunately, she was able to nap every day with her baby while her older daughter went to school. When the drug haze wore off, she became aware of lively chatter and laughter echoing in the hallways. A new life opened up to Stacy, filled with Bible studies, outpatient drug treatment, and lots of counseling. As time went on, stable routines replaced the chaos in her life.

For her girls, life at the shelter was an adventure. They enjoyed being with other children in childcare and kid's activities. Her outgoing seven-year-old made friends with everyone, and her baby naturally attracted attention because all the women wanted to hold her.

LIFE AT THE SHELTER

Sometimes living at the shelter intimidated Stacy. She often asked herself, *Why am I different from some of these folks?* Gradually she realized that she came from a different culture, a middleclass culture. She had succeeded in school settings and work settings. Many of the women came from a culture of poverty that showed up in their behaviors. Often ladies cut in front of her in the breakfast line for milk.

This is ridiculous! This isn't how it's supposed to be! she fumed to herself. Soon she learned to be flexible enough to laugh and cut in line too.

Stacy adapted to the rules at the shelter: no TV or food in your room, no loud music, and make your bed every day. She also learned to show up early on pizza night if she wanted anything to eat. Pizza was the favorite food, so everyone showed up to eat when pizza was served.

Life at the shelter wasn't all work and no play. Many of the women had forgotten how to have fun, since 90 percent were addicted to a drug or alcohol, and the same percentage had come from abusive relationships or had been victims of domestic abuse. To relax and laugh, Stacy joined with other residents and staff in karaoke sings, talent shows, picnics, and game nights. Stacy believes it wasn't only the program that changed her; it was also relationship—being with others, sharing problems, victories, and having fun together.

God's Promise

Because Seattle's UGM is a Christian recovery program, the staff required Stacy to attend certain Bible studies. She tried to avoid one loud African-American leader who yelled. One week she had no other choice but to go to that class.

Pacing back and forth the teacher screamed Scripture from Isaiah 40.

> Have you never heard?
>> Have you never understood?
> The Lord is the everlasting God,
>> the Creator of all the earth.
> He never grows weak or weary.
>> No one can measure the depths of his understanding.
> He gives power to the weak
>> and strength to the powerless.
> Even youths will become weak and tired,
>> and young men will fall in exhaustion.
> But those who trust in the Lord will find new strength.
>> They will soar high on wings like eagles.
> They will run and not grow weary.
>> They will walk and not faint. [26]

Mesmerized, as if hearing God's words for the first time, Stacy listened. God wanted those Scriptures screamed at her that day. She clung to the words, convinced she couldn't quit drugs and change her life on her own, but God promised to carry her through it with his strength.

"I saw myself as I really was—a mess but loved and cherished by God."

SONRISE HOUSE

After four months at the shelter, Stacy and her daughters moved to Seattle's UGM Sonrise House, a transitional facility for graduates of the recovery program. Here her third daughter, a cuddly, quiet, but alert baby was born. Once again, she was immersed in the fresh smell of baby powder on her newborn's soft skin. Shortly after that, Stacy needed current job experience, so she volunteered at Seattle's UGM and fell in love with the work. UGM hired her as a receptionist, then office manager, and eventually, administrative assistant. The former director, Gloria Hall, saw lots of potential in Stacy and mentored her to take over as director.

"I never envisioned working at a shelter, but God had a plan," Stacy reflects.

DIRECTOR OF HOPE PLACE

In 2007, eight years after Stacy Cleveland first sought refuge at the shelter, she became the new director. The Women and Children's Shelter moved to a new building in 2009 with twice as much space to house those in need. They named it Hope Place.

More recently she became Director of Women and Children's Ministries overseeing two additional emergency shelters and a transitional-housing location.

Besides community meetings every day with all the women, children and staff, Stacy also teaches a class, screens women for intake, gives tours, speaks to outside groups, and manages a budget of over one million dollars. Being the director has its challenges. "I don't have all the answers because I'm the director," she says. "There are days when not everyone likes me!"

When Stacy Cleveland shares her story with the residents, she wants them to know they're not alone in their struggles. The ladies can't believe that their poised, serene director was just like them not too many years ago. One woman asked to see a "before" picture. As Stacy passed around a photo of a young woman with a lost look in her eyes, the room got quiet. The ladies murmured in disbelief. That photo made a deep impression on them.

"I tell the women the blessing of addiction is that we see our own brokenness. We're on display; we see our need, and we can't do this on our own."

REWARDS

Every day Stacy Cleveland sees God show up in amazing ways. Women enter the shelter just trying to make it through the day, so it excites her to see them dream about the future. At Seattle's UGM there's a 70 percent success rate among women recovering from addiction—much higher than in other recovery programs. Most women transform their lives, grab on to newfound hope, and some even accept Christ into their lives.

Not long ago, a woman entered the program but experienced crying jags and trips to the hospital for medical detox. Stacy doubted the woman would succeed. As the weeks went by, the woman adjusted and blossomed. "Being proved wrong is one of my great rewards," said Stacy, thinking about that incident. "I believe no one is beyond hope. I don't think there is anyone beyond the reach of God. We have hope. That's why we're here."

A FULL LIFE

Besides being the director of Women and Children's Ministries, Stacy Cleveland is also a busy mom and wife. She met Scott Cleveland, who also works at Seattle's Union Gospel Mission, married him in 2003, and they had another daughter. With four daughters, most evenings she helps with homework. She and her husband recently bought a home, and they plan to fill it with their family and pets. Stacy intentionally carves out time for her family. "I love spending time with my girls. I enjoy them so, so much."

Love for her girls was the key factor in Stacy's recovery from drugs and homelessness. It was her desire for a better life for her daughters that caused her to make the initial phone call to Seattle's Union Gospel Mission. When she entered the shelter, even the staff noticed her determination to change. As she accepted responsibility in her life, she gathered support around her and reconnected with the Lord. Now Stacy believes in "taking off my mask and being real" about her problems and her past. She shares things that she's not proud of because it encourages others. She wants program residents to know they're not the only ones with problems and they *can* overcome them with God's help.

"It gives people hope, and that's what it's all about!"

Notable Quotable

"I believe no one is beyond hope. I don't think
there is anyone beyond the reach of God.
We have hope. That's why we're here."
– Stacy Cleveland

Points to Remember

- Be responsible for your choices.
- Know that you are not alone in your problems.
- Be accountable to someone for your actions and decisions.
- Lean on God's strength to overcome your weaknesses.
- Remember you are loved and cherished by God.

Take Action

1. When Stacy Cleveland entered Seattle's Union Gospel Mission shelter, it was her first step in taking responsibility for her choices that led to drug abuse and homelessness. Do you take responsibility for your own behavior? How much effort are you willing to put into being more responsible?
2. Being in relationship with other women who shared struggles and victories helped Stacy through recovery. When you feel alone in your problems do you search for support?
3. How willing are you to be accountable to one other person for your actions and decisions?

4. Have you ever come to a place in your life where your strength wasn't enough to overcome your problems? Where did you find your strength?
5. How can you know for sure that you are loved and cherished by God?

To Learn More about Stacy Cleveland and Seattle's Union Gospel Mission

Hope Place, Seattle's Union Gospel Mission's Women and Children's Shelter: www.ugm.org

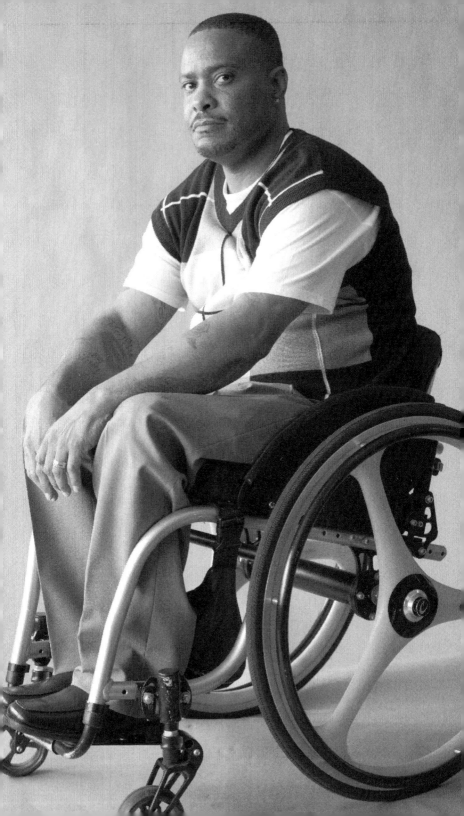

CHAPTER 8

SECRET NUMBER EIGHT: GIVE PEACE A CHANCE

THE STORY OF ERIC GIBSON

The car crawled down the street of South Central Los Angeles. From the open window a gang member fired a powerful Magnum .357 pistol. His prey was rival gang member, twenty-five-year-old Eric Gibson.

Boom! Boom! Boom!

The sound blasted through the streets. Trees shook. Squawking birds flew in all directions. One bullet hit a thirteen-year-old girl. With her last breath she screamed and then died. Five bullets struck Eric in the back. He collapsed on the pavement.

His brother rushed to him. "Man, you're shot!" he cried. "Don't move!"

No pain. Eric felt only burning sensations where the bullets pierced his back. In the distance he heard police and ambulance sirens. He emptied his pockets quickly, took off his jewelry and passed his gun to his brother. The approaching sirens wailed in the cool October evening air.

In the ambulance, Eric first thought about his four little children that he didn't want to leave fatherless. Then he thought about friends who had been shot and died. Sobered by the possibility of his own death, he prayed.

"God, if you save my life, I promise to dedicate the rest of my life to stop some of this mess I'm involved in."[27]

Eric Gibson survived the 1993 gang-retaliation drive-by shooting, but sustained a spinal cord injury that left him paralyzed and in a wheelchair. He kept his promise to God, overcame the pull to reenter gang life, and established himself in business selling medical supplies. Yet his real mission was to help others—those in wheelchairs and kids in the inner city. He committed his life to the prevention of violence. Today he wheels into schools and rehabilitation and detention centers, speaking to teens about drugs, peer pressure and gang violence. As he shares his story, he hopes it will prevent kids from joining gangs and going through what he did.

From the Country to the City

Eric Gibson grew up in rural Mississippi with his mom, five brothers, and a sister. His three older brothers lived with his grandparents, who adopted them. Eric never had a father figure and only later in life realized how much it affected him and the decisions he made.

When he was twelve, Eric's family moved to Los Angeles for better opportunities. To Eric, LA meant Disneyland and Hollywood, the place where movies were made, so he was excited to move. However, as he stepped off the Greyhound bus in downtown LA, he saw dirty homeless people on the street and graffiti scrawled across the walls. "I thought for a minute my momma had taken us to hell!" Eric said later. Country life in Mississippi hadn't exposed him to big city poverty or crime and what he saw scared him. Fortunately, his family settled in another part of the city. Just a "young, country boy" trying to fit in, Eric hung out with the guys who lived in his community. "I was ready to get involved with anybody and anything that was going on," he remembers. "As we got older, the crews that we used to run with turned into gangs."

In his neighborhood, the only "successful" people were drug dealers who wore expensive clothes, drove shiny new BMWs, and surrounded themselves with three or four beautiful girls at a time. As a young teen, Eric looked at them and said "I want that!" The lifestyle was very attractive to him and he wanted the attention that it promised him.

Gang Life

By age fifteen, Eric was selling drugs and robbing people. His gang, the Fruit Town Brims, an offshoot of the Bloods, became a brotherhood whose members protected each other and their territory.

Police first arrested Eric when he was seventeen. He spent nine months in juvenile detention at Camp Paige, California, a place he compared to Disneyland. He ate very well, exercised in a huge well-equipped gym, lived in a dorm instead of a cell, and got passes for good behavior to attend the movies or go home on weekends. At Camp Paige he finished his high school diploma and became a teacher's assistant. When Eric left he had no fear of jail because he thought he knew what it was like. "It didn't rehabilitate me; it just took me out of my element for a while," Eric later reflected. "I went right back to selling drugs and robbing people."

Eric wanted money—lots of easy money—and lots of women. The gang life gave him that. The adrenaline rush of constant danger and the strong bonds he formed with other members hooked him, too. His gang became his protection, unconditional support, and family. When Eric was only eighteen, he woke up every morning in his own apartment and pulled on his designer jeans and white tee-shirt. He added a red belt and red shoes to show he belonged to a gang affiliated with the Bloods. He hung a heavy gold chain around his neck and slipped a diamond-studded gold watch on his wrist. Then he drove his new car to a house in another neighborhood where he sold cocaine and marijuana all day long to a steady stream of customers.

He earned the title "OG" or "Original Gangster" at twenty-five because he'd survived in the gang for ten years. He moved up to management where his job involved keeping the neighborhood flowing with drugs. Even though four of his brothers had already been shot, and despite the many friends he knew who ended up injured or dead, Eric didn't think *he* would be shot. Eric now explains, I thought "That will never happen to me!"

Then the drive-by shooting took place.

IN THE HOSPITAL AND REHABILITATION

After surgery in the hospital, Eric learned that three bullets had passed straight through him without injuring any of his vital organs. But two bullets were still lodged inside him. One had hit his spinal cord (a T-12 incomplete injury), paralyzing him from the waist down, but he still had some feeling and movement in both legs.

When his wounds healed, he spent nine weeks in a rehabilitation hospital learning how to live his life in a wheelchair. His arms ached from the many transfers he made daily using his upper body strength to lift his whole body. He lifted himself from his chair onto a sofa, in and out of a car, onto the toilet, into the shower, and in and out of bed. He learned how to drive his car using hand controls. The worst thing was using a catheter to empty his bladder. Yet Eric remained positive and determined not to feel sorry for himself, even when he was told he wouldn't walk again. "Whatever God left me with, I was gonna use it. If he took my legs, I'd use my arms," Eric said later.

When a social worker visited him and asked him if he had thoughts of suicide due to his injury, it angered Eric. "Lady," he said, "I'm not trying to kill myself, so you can just go on about your business!"

Once out of rehabilitation, Eric returned to his apartment and leaned on his family and his girlfriend for help and support. But life in the real world hit him hard. Embarrassed by his paralysis, he avoided friends. His bowel and bladder accidents depressed him, and he didn't want to leave his apartment. He felt overwhelmed with all the changes he had to make and discouraged by the physical barriers of stairs and curbs he faced every day in a wheelchair. For months he woke up, ate, smoked marijuana, and watched TV. He didn't need *TV Guide* because he memorized the schedule. Soon his money dwindled, and he went back to selling drugs, the only thing he knew how to do. The police arrested him again, and he spent two long, miserable days in jail—"not a comfortable place for someone in a wheelchair." That was Eric's wakeup call.

Remembering that time, Eric said, "I told myself I'll never go back to jail. I won't sell dope anymore, and I don't want to be in a gang anymore. I said to myself 'I'm through with all of this!'"

Motivation to Change

With the help of another wheelchair-bound friend, Glenford Herbert, Eric moved into a wheelchair-accessible apartment in Marina Del Rey near the Pacific Ocean. He made a clean break with his old friends in the gang and got into a business selling medical supplies, his first legitimate income. Glenford invited Eric to church, but Eric didn't take it seriously.

One day Glenford looked at Eric and said, "Boy, you're still doing stupid stuff! Grow up, Eric. Save some money, find one girl, and stop dressing in gang colors!"

Eric started to make gradual but definite changes in his life. When Glenford died suddenly from heart disease, Eric was devastated. From that point on, Eric sought to do what God wanted him to do. He returned to his childhood faith, involved himself in ministries at his church, spent more time with his children, counseled the newly injured at Rancho Los Amigos Rehabilitation Center in LA, and began speaking about ways to stop violence.

New Opportunities

Since Eric had some feeling in both legs, his physical therapist sent him to another rehabilitation center that taught him to "walk" with specialty braces. He traveled all over the world demonstrating these braces and wore them as a torch bearer in the 1996 Paralympics in Atlanta. At one of his presentations, he met a man who persuaded him to serve on the National Spinal Cord Injury Association Board in Washington, D.C. Eric became the second black man to serve on the board, the first in forty-eight years.

Sitting around a boardroom table with fifty doctors, lawyers, accountants, and other professionals, Eric felt "scared to death like a church-house mouse." He didn't know what to say or do. He thought of himself as the ex-gang member from LA, but the board members befriended him and listened to his ideas about stopping gang violence that led to so many spinal cord injuries. Doors continued to open for Eric. He met more influential people, magazines interviewed him, and he appeared on television.

The Christopher and Dana Reeves Foundation asked him to be an ambassador and gave him grant money for speaking in schools, at community events, and in rehabilitation facilities.

Striving to be taken seriously, Eric pursued a two-year program at UCLA for certification in alcohol and drug abuse counseling, and another certificate in violence prevention and intervention from the Los Angeles Sheriff's Department.

Peace Talks

Several times a week, Eric rolls into schools, sometimes in his everyday chair, sometimes with his twenty-inch fancy chrome spinner rims. "My chair is a part of who I am, so I want it to look nice," he says.

He answers questions like, "Where did you get those rims?" and "Can you do wheelies in your chair?" Then he talks to kids about his injury, gangs, and drugs.

"Once you're in a gang, you're always a target. When you want to quit, there's no commercial that comes out saying 'Hey, I'm Eric Gibson and I'm not in a gang anymore, so don't bother me!'"

He tells them bluntly that drugs and alcohol play a big part in gangs because members need to alter their brains before they go out and kill somebody.

"What do you do when you're on your way home from school and a gangbanger stops you and pulls a gun on you?" They ask, "Hey, where are you from? What gang are you from?"

"Don't run," Eric tells his audience. "They'll think you're guilty and shoot you. Put your hands up in the air and say, 'Hey man, I do not have anything to do with gangs. I don't even know what you're saying. I'm just on my way home from school.'"

Eric presents several workshops, some on gangs and drugs, and others on teen dating, teen pregnancy, and one designed for parents of inner-city teens. His current passion is producing public service announcements on his YouTube channel.

In one he says to kids: "Choose life instead of death. Choose college instead of prison. Choose walking instead of rolling in a wheelchair. Help us stop violence in our community!"

Eric often hears from kids who listened to his message and changed their lives. Once while Eric was pumping gas, a teen recognized him from a speech he gave in his class.

"I know how to handle myself now," the teen told him. "I don't want to be a gang member."

Another time in a grocery store, a different boy recognized him. The young man's mother thanked Eric because her son had changed his life, and he wasn't involved in gang activity anymore.

BLESSINGS

In his youth, money had meant a lot to Eric. Now he says, "My paycheck comes from my blessings." One of those blessings is his family, the children he almost let slip away. His four children all have different mothers, but the children think of themselves as one family.

On a recent Father's Day, Eric gathered his wife and family around him at a Cajun restaurant. "I do love you," Eric told them. "I was young and dumb in my past. I'm sorry for the time I lost with you, but we still have time to be together." His family is his constant support, and they motivate him to live a good life, and be a role model for his beloved grandchildren.

ERIC TODAY

In 2014 Eric Gibson moved to Arizona and opened a business, Alexander Home Healthcare, in Fort Collins, Colorado. He continues to teach those recently disabled by spinal cord injuries and speaks in his new Arizona community about violence prevention.

"This Is the Life That Was Chosen for Me"

After twenty-one years in a wheelchair, Eric Gibson can now say that his spinal cord injury has blessed him. Without it he would probably be in prison or dead. Eric never asked the question, "Why me?" but rather, "Why not me?" He feels God allowed him to suffer this injury because he knew Eric could handle it. God is using Eric to teach peaceful solutions to resolve violence. "I pray every day about what God wants me to do. I ask God every day to use me."

Another level of healing took place when Eric recently contacted the family of the girl who was killed in the same drive-by shooting. Her name was Arriana Rodriguez. Since Eric was one of the last people to see her alive, Eric explained to her family exactly what happened on that fateful day that changed his life and took Arriana's. As the family cried with Eric, it brought them so much healing that they told him, "We are making you part of our family!" After many years, Eric made peace with all the events of that tragic day in his past.

From gang member to peacemaker, from hurting people to helping people, Eric Gibson overcame his past, his violent lifestyle, and his attitude about his paralysis. Day by day he found peace with God, peace with himself, and peace with others. He says, "There is no other life that I would choose to live than the one I live right now."

Notable Quotable

"There is no other life that I would choose to
live than the one I live right now."
– Eric Gibson

Points to Remember

- Break away from bad or negative influences in your life.
- Make peace with your past.
- Be a peacemaker.
- Be open to people and opportunities that will help you.
- Ask God to use you every day.

Take Action

1. Eric Gibson's neighborhood influenced him in a negative way, but he took steps to overcome those negative peer networks. He moved to another community, went into business selling medical supplies, and made new friends. What negative influences can you change in your life?
2. Eric made peace with his past, his mistakes, and those he had hurt. What part of your life needs peace?
3. What opportunities do you have to be a peacemaker?
4. How open are you to receiving help from others?
5. How often do you ask God to use you?

To Learn More about Eric K. Gibson and Spinal Cord Injuries

Life Coach, Prevention & Intervention Specialist; Life Medical Homecare Urological Specialist; and guidance and support for people with spinal cord injuries: www.wheelchair-with-a-purpose.com

His videos: www.youtube.com/user/MrEricgibson100

Ambassador for the Christopher & Dana Reeve Foundation: www.christopherreeve.org

CHAPTER 9

SECRET NUMBER NINE: DEVELOP A CARING HEART

THE STORY OF GIGI DEVINE MURFITT

A newborn's raspy cry filled the delivery room. Everyone else was eerily quiet. Gigi Murfitt didn't hear the usual delivery room chatter or congratulations about her baby. Instead she heard the doctor say "Oh, oh, we have some problems."[28]

Gigi's first look at her newborn son, Gabriel, left her in shock. He didn't have arms, only short fatty tissue to which his hands were attached. From deep within her, a sob erupted that she couldn't control. Her husband, Steve, calmed her as the nurse quickly cleaned and swaddled Gabe and handed him to Gigi. Through her tears, she kissed him on his nose and quieted his newborn cries. As she looked into his beautiful blue eyes and touched his tender skin, love for her baby consumed her. In that moment she knew that God would help her through this tragedy. Then the nurse whisked Gabe away to test him for life-threatening problems.

Gabe was born with congenital birth defects. His three-inch arms are missing the radius and ulna bones of the forearms, and his legs are fused at a forty-five degree angle to his knees. He also has a hearing loss because bone is covering the ear canals—a condition Gigi learned about later.

And so began Gigi's challenging years as a caregiver to a special-needs child. She became Gabe's arms and legs, his emotional support, and his cheerleader. She prepared him for life and learned with him how to handle difficulties. All the while she quietly carried his hurts of loneliness and rejection. Gigi developed a very close bond with Gabe, but then she released him so he could assert his own independence.

Gabe, now in his twenties, is a capable, optimistic young man, with an associate's degree. He is a motivational speaker in schools and the author of a book about his life, *My Message is C.L.E.A.R.*

"I am so proud of Gabe," says Gigi, "and how he has championed through this life in an unusually shaped body."

GROWING UP IN MONTANA

Gigi Devine grew up in Anaconda, a small copper mining town in the mountains of southwest Montana. She was the eighth of ten children.

"I loved growing up in Montana where family ties were important and everyone looked out for their neighbor," Gigi remembers. "The downside of that was everyone looked out for their neighbor! There was not much getting away with anything, because someone would inform our mom."

When Gigi was only seven, her father died from cancer. Her mother assumed the responsibility of raising and providing for their large family. Even though her mom had a spinal injury and walked with a severe limp, she taught junior high school English and instilled in her ten children the desire to overcome obstacles and live their lives to the fullest.

After Gigi Devine received her college degree in accounting, she worked as an oil and gas accountant. A few years later she married Steve Murfitt, whom she had met on the ski slopes in Montana. Their first child, Zane, was born in Dallas, Texas. With a desire to be closer to family, they moved to Seattle, where many of their siblings lived.

GABE'S BIRTH

Gigi's second pregnancy was normal with no complications. Even an ultrasound appeared normal, so nothing prepared her for a baby with severe birth defects. Her days in the hospital after Gabe's birth are hazy to her now. She and Steve saw many doctors and specialists, and they watched Gabe undergo a multitude of tests. Despite all their worries about the kind of life he would live, they were grateful that he had no life-threatening issues and he showed no signs of brain damage.

Later, Gigi and Steve realized the extent of Gabe's deformities. At birth his legs were pulled into a fetal position, but X-rays showed they were actually fused at the knee. Once they had hoped that Gabe's legs would straighten and he would be able to walk normally, but a doctor's blunt diagnosis told them otherwise.

"You'll never have to buy him shoes," the doctor quipped.

That comment knocked the air out of Gigi like a surprise punch. Tears spilled from her eyes as the cruel reality hit her. She broke down and cried openly about her baby's misshapen body.

A NEW PERSPECTIVE

In the weeks after Gabe's birth, Gigi muddled around in a fog, unable to focus on her role as the mother of a disabled child. Fear, uncertainty and loneliness crushed her. Gradually, with the support of friends, family, and their prayers, she changed her perspective.

"Yes, I had arrived at a different place than I had planned, but God soon opened my eyes to the beauty of my new surroundings."[29]

On a trip with friends to a tulip festival, Gigi received reassurance about others' acceptance of Gabe's different body. An eight-year-old friend, Kellie, and her sister, Jaimie, were excited to see the new baby.

"Can I please hold Gabe?" Kellie asked.[30]

Gigi unwrapped tiny Gabe from his blankets, exposing his deformed arms. She placed him gently on Kellie's lap, expecting the young girls to gasp, but instead they admired him.

"He has such long eyelashes," Jaimie said. "And his eyes are so blue."

That same day, Gigi read a letter from Dianne, the girls' mom. Dianne reminded Gigi that Gabe was "fearfully and wonderfully made" and that God had knit him together in her womb. Those words touched Gigi's broken heart as though God were speaking directly to her. Gigi knew then that Gabe was not a mistake as her fears as a mother had made her believe.

She recalls, "I knew then that Gabe was designed especially by God in love. Oh, how I needed to hear this truth!"[31]

Gabe's birth compelled Gigi to seek support and fellowship in a Bible-believing church. She drank in God's Word like a thirsty wanderer. Thinking about it now, she says, "I've had to rely on God to give me strength for the journey."[32]

A WORKING MOTHER

Gigi Murfitt agonized about going back to work and leaving both of her boys in daycare. *Would a stranger be able to deal with Gabe's unique needs?* she wondered. But Steve's company refused to insure Gabe, so she needed to work for medical coverage. Fortunately, she found a nanny who loved her boys and gave them good care.

So, busy Gigi navigated the system of doctors and accepted the challenges of teaching Gabe to adapt to life. A chubby-cheeked baby with an engaging smile and a sweet disposition, Gabe eagerly learned. Without thumbs on his hands, and lacking legs that could walk, he held a bottle with his feet, swung on his stomach on playground swings, and hopped on his bottom to get around.

When Gabe was two years old, doctors recommended the use of an electric wheelchair. Gabe needed mobility to be more independent and play with other children. However, the price tag astounded the Murfitts—over twenty thousand dollars! Family and friends heard about their need and organized several fundraising events that paid for the chair as well as a van to transport it

Soon Gabe was driving a bright blue "Turbo Bobcat" wheelchair with a joystick similar to the ones used with video games. His "wheels" came equipped with an elevator in the seat to lower him to the ground so he could hop off.

Struggling with Reality

As Gabe grew older, Gigi watched her boys connect through sports. They played football together with helmets and shoulder pads. Zane played on his knees so he would be the same height as his younger brother. He played catch with Gabe and taught him how to dribble a basketball and kick a soccer ball. Gabe learned a lot about sports when he sat on the sidelines and watched his older brother play.

One morning when Gigi and her boys pulled into the school parking lot, third-grader Zane jumped out of the van to play with friends.

As Gigi was getting out the wheelchair, kindergartener Gabe said, "I don't want to take my wheelchair to school today. I want to run onto the playground like Zane. Why do I have to use a wheelchair?"[33]

"You'll always have a wheelchair, Gabe," answered Gigi. "It's the way you get around."

"What? You mean when I'm in third grade like Zane, I won't have long legs and be able to run like him? Are my arms going to grow long like his?"

Gigi looked at him and gently said, "No Gabe. You're missing bones in your arms. They aren't going to grow. The bones in your legs are fused together. I'm sorry, Honey, but unless God gives us a miracle, they won't grow long like Zane's."

Gigi reached over to hug a tearful Gabe, and they both cried. They sat in the van for a long time, overwhelmed with emotion.

Over the next several months, Gigi and Steve talked with Gabe about his feelings and disability. They urged him to make the best of the body God had given him. They affirmed that God planned to use Gabe for mighty things.

"Truly understanding that God has a good plan for us has been the most important part of raising Gabe." Gigi said later. "We don't focus on his disability. Instead we encourage him to trust that God's plan for him is good. We know he will find a way to succeed."[34]

Gabe in Challenger Baseball and School

Gabe wanted to play baseball like his older brother, so Gigi and Steve discovered Challenger Little League where children with physical and mental challenges experience the thrill of playing baseball and even wearing uniforms just like other Little Leaguers. Gabe joined when he was six years old, and Steve ended up coaching their team for nineteen years.

Gigi cheered as Gabe batted, hopped around the bases, and played outfield. His newfound confidence warmed her heart.

She later explained, "Our involvement in this organization was very healing for us because it gave us a glimpse of an activity Gabe could do instead of the reminders of all the things his unique body could not do."[35]

Gigi also guided Gabe through the hurdles of elementary school. While para-educators assisted him in the classroom, Gigi learned when to help him and when to let him assert himself at home. Gabe held his books by balancing them on one foot and one knee. He wrote by holding a pencil or pen between his pointer and middle fingers. Even with his short arms, he became the fastest typist on the keyboard in his elementary school.

Basketball and Publicity

In junior high, Gabe joined the Leota Lions basketball team. The coach and the team accommodated Gabe, who stood only three feet tall with three-inch arms, by slowing the game to let him play.

At their last game, Seattle's *King 5 News* filmed and interviewed Gabe and the team and then aired the story, "Gabe, the Lionhearted," during its evening news segment. Then the *Seattle Times* wrote a feature story on Gabe. Requests for interviews kept pouring in. *Good Morning America* sent a camera crew that followed Gabe around for three days. Then the *Oprah Winfrey Show* filmed Gabe at his home and flew the Murfitt family to Chicago for the taping of a show. The whole family was on stage with Oprah when she introduced Gabe as a real-life superhero. The entire audience stood and applauded. Overwhelmed, Gigi wiped her tears away, all the while worrying about messing up her makeup at such an important moment.

High School Challenges

High school brought more challenges for Gabe, especially in his social life. His friends changed, and he no longer received invitations to parties or movies or just to hang out.

Gigi saw and felt his loneliness. It was heart-wrenching for her to watch Gabe's isolation, but she encouraged him to stay positive and hope for the best. They talked it out and learned how to handle those difficult times together. When Gigi didn't know what to do or say to ease Gabe's pain, she took the matter to God and trusted him to show her the way.

TYRANNOSAURUS REX

A few years ago, while enjoying a Mother's Day brunch at an Anthony's restaurant the Murfitts noticed a little boy staring wide-eyed at Gabe then hiding his face.

"Is that boy a *T. rex*, Mother?" he asked innocently but loudly enough for the Murfitts to hear.[36]

Gigi remembers the surprised look on Gabe's face as he said, "Did that boy just call me a prehistoric dinosaur? Well, you can't blame him. Short arms. Bent crooked legs. I do sort of look *T. rex*ish!"

Then Gabe's family burst out laughing.

The child's mother reddened, fumbled with her napkin, and apologized for her son's comment.

"Do you want to come over and talk?" Gabe asked the little boy.

The boy nodded and approached Gabe.

"I may have short arms, but I don't have gnarly teeth like a *T. rex*. And I sure won't bite your head off like a ferocious dinosaur would!" said Gabe.

The conversation continued as the little boy and his family grew comfortable with Gabe's appearance. Gabe explained that he was born with short arms and bent legs, and even though he might look different, he really was not that different from everyone else.

The whole family learned a lesson that day. By inviting questions and responding in kindness, others discovered that disabilities aren't scary.

Gabriel's Foundation of Hope

A short time later, Gigi and Steve attended a Watoto Children's Choir concert. The choir travels throughout the world raising funds for the fifty million children in Africa orphaned by HIV/AIDS, war, poverty, and disease.

Inspired by the concert, Gigi and Steve talked about their desire to help the disabled and their families in a similar way. Their plan became a reality, and Gabriel's Foundation of Hope was born. So far the foundation has given scholarships to students in the special-needs field, money to build a wheelchair access ramp to a house, and a laptop and voice software for another boy with arms like Gabe's. Their foundation also supplies food, gift cards, and other monetary help to families of the disabled.

A New Season

In 2010 Gigi Devine Murfitt authored a book, *Caregivers' Devotions to Go* and coauthored a book with Gabe in 2012, *My Message is C.L.E.A.R.* She is a past president and treasurer of Northwest Christian Writers Association and a speaker who encourages others with her journey of raising a child with birth defects while trusting God for her every need. She's frequently in the audience when Gabe speaks at schools and churches.

She says, "I cry almost every time he speaks as I watch the young kids learn from him and share with him how much he inspired them. I believe this is what God has called him to do, and I know it will continue to bless thousands."

It's a deeply satisfying time for Gigi after overcoming the stigma of having a disabled child and dealing with social loneliness, isolation, and fears of Gabe not being accepted. She took on every new challenge as a caregiver with faith and a positive outlook, refusing to focus on Gabe's disability. Instead, she trusted God for Gabe's future and her own strength.

Gigi's role as a caregiver is changing as she transitions to a new season in her life. She now has a granddaughter and hopes to have more grandchildren to spoil as they "ruffle the feathers" in her empty nest.

NOTABLE QUOTABLE

"I had arrived at a different place than
I had planned, but God soon opened my eyes
to the beauty of my new surroundings."
– Gigi Devine Murfitt

POINTS TO REMEMBER

- Acknowledge your positive and negative emotions.
- Reach out to others for encouragement.
- Accept each new challenge.
- Ask God to show you his perspective on your problems.
- Develop a caring heart.

TAKE ACTION

1. It helped Gigi to express her emotions about raising a special-needs child. How open are you to communicating your emotions in a positive way?
2. Reaching out to others was vital for Gigi in times of loneliness and isolation. How do you seek encouragement from others who can help you?
3. Do you bemoan the loss of comfort or routine when faced with a new challenge? How easily do you accept new challenges?
4. How often do you ask God to reveal his perspective on your situation?
5. Years of caring for her sons cultivated a caring heart in Gigi. How can you develop a caring heart?

To Learn More about Gigi Devine Murfitt and Gabriel's Foundation of Hope

Gigi's website: www.GigiMurfitt.com

Gabriel's Foundation of Hope: www.GabesHope.org

Gigi's books:

Caregivers' Devotions to Go (Orange, CA: Extreme Diva Media, Inc., 2010).

My Message is C.L.E.A.R.: Hope and Strength in the Face of Life's Greatest Adversities. Coauthored with Gabe Murfitt (Woodinville, WA: Gabriel's Foundation of Hope, 2012).

CHAPTER 10

SECRET NUMBER TEN: GOD GIVES SECOND CHANCES

THE STORY OF JOSH HAMILTON

"Ham-il-ton! Ham-il-ton! MVP!" Thousands of fans chanted the name. The roar of the crowd rolled through the Rangers' ballpark in Arlington, Texas. Josh Hamilton stepped up to the platform to receive the American League Championship Series (ALCS) Most Valuable Player award.

The fans yelled louder. "Ham-il-ton! Ham-il-ton! MVP!"

Later in an interview, Josh Hamilton remembered that moment—the thousands of fans, the thundering noise, the Rangers' American League victory over the Yankees—and said, "It's just awesome to think about where I am at this moment and where I was."[37]

Not so long ago, the chants from the fans were different. "Josh smokes crack! Josh is a drug addict!"[38]

Playing in the outfield between innings, Josh spun around to face one heckler. With arms outstretched he smiled and yelled back, "Tell me something I don't know!"[39]

Josh Hamilton, now a leftfielder with the Los Angeles Angels, overcame a drug addiction that almost cost him his career in baseball, his family, and his very life. Major League Baseball had banned him from playing for four years because he repeatedly tested positive for drugs. Those years of addiction are a blur to him now.

THE EARLY YEARS

Josh Hamilton grew up playing baseball in Raleigh, North Carolina. At the age of six, he threw harder and hit farther than other kids his age. Josh's teammates ducked when he threw the ball, so there was little hope of playing a ballgame. Parents worried Josh would injure their kids, so coaches politely removed him from a coach-pitch team. He moved up to a Little League team of twelve-year olds. Six years younger than his teammates, he threw a fifty-mile-per-hour ball and hit homeruns. Baseball was already his life, and he had talent.

In high school, classmates knew Josh as "the nice baseball player" because he found good in everybody. He mingled easily with all groups—the jocks, the stoners, the brainy kids, and special education students—and was well-liked by all. They nicknamed him "Hambone" and "Hammer." Josh wanted nothing to interfere with his baseball ambitions and his strenuous training, so he didn't drink or smoke. Classmates respected that.

By his senior year, left-handed Josh ranked as one of the top five high-school players in the country. As a pitcher, he threw a ninety-six-mile-per-hour ball. As an outfielder, he had a smooth, quick stride and a strong arm that hurled a ball from the outfield wall to home plate. Besides that, Josh hit with power and ran like the wind. His high school coach hailed Josh as better at baseball than anyone the coach had seen in high school or college. In his senior year, Josh was named High School Player of the Year by *Baseball America* and Amateur Player of the Year by USA Baseball.

Josh Hamilton dazzled the baseball world with his incredible talent. Everyone thought he could be the next Mickey Mantle. While other top baseball players talked with college coaches, Josh drew the attention of professional scouts and agents. Josh heard them say: "The ball just sounds different coming off his bat."[40] "That's one of the greatest swings I've ever seen." "That's Josh Hamilton; he's going to make it big someday."

When Josh graduated from high school in 1999, the Major League drafted him as first pick. The Tampa Bay Devil Rays paid him an amazing $3.96 million as a signing bonus—almost 4 four million dollars at age eighteen.

Drugs and the Minor Leagues

Josh Hamilton started his baseball career in the minor leagues. He traveled with his parents to practices and kissed his mom before each game. He dreamed of moving up to play Major League Baseball and being inducted into the Hall of Fame. However, a car accident in 2001 involving Josh and his parents suddenly changed his plans. His parents returned home to recover from their injuries, leaving Josh on his own with an injured back.

A short time later, Josh injured his leg during a game, sidelining him from playing baseball. Lonely, with time on his hands and money—a lot of money—Josh headed to the tattoo parlor. He sat in a chair hour after hour and watched the designs as ink decorated his skin. The "tattoo guys" soon became his friends.

"They weren't bad people," he recalls. "They just did bad things."[41] He took his first drink ever with his buddies at a strip club, and that same night they introduced him to cocaine. Josh now admits that his need for acceptance and friends, and the effects of alcohol lowering his resistance, all played a role in his decision to try cocaine.

Josh played only twenty-seven games in 2001. The next season he suffered more injuries, which led to more free time, which led to more drugs. The cycle of relapses, rehabilitation, and more relapses spun him around and around. Eventually, Major League Baseball suspended him for failing drug tests.

During that time, from 2003 until 2006, he played very few baseball games. He barely lifted a bat for batting practice. In his heart, Josh Hamilton believed he would never play baseball again. His rare talent was wasting away.

ADDICTION

Drug addiction consumed his thoughts. "It controlled my life. Everything I did seemed to revolve around it; wanting it, getting it, using it, wanting it all over again. It's the hamster wheel of drug abuse: You keep running, you get nowhere."[42]

Cocaine and booze filled his days and nights. Hallucinations and paranoia clouded his mind. One time he thought he saw a SWAT team storming his house, coming to arrest him. His imagination ran wild until he realized it was only a salesman knocking at the door.

Desperate for drugs, Josh pawned his wife's wedding ring. (He married in 2004.) He even sold a treasured Minor League championship ring to buy crack. One summer he spent one hundred thousand dollars on drugs. Many days he forgot to eat, so he lost weight quickly, sometimes fifteen pounds a week. He went from a muscular 235 pounds to a thin and weak 180 pounds.

During this dark period, he hung out at a tattoo parlor and now has twenty-six tattoos covering his body. One of them is a demon with no eyes, a symbol of a soulless being. Looking back, Josh admits he felt like that—a man with no soul, an empty shell.

Josh Hamilton stumbled through a fog-world, glassy-eyed and mumbling. Many nights he passed out in strange places. He woke up dirty, sweaty, and craving more drugs. His body twitched, his palms sweat, and his heart hammered in his chest. He coughed up black matter from his lungs. He came close to overdosing and made several trips to the emergency room. Those closest to him wondered how much abuse his body could take. Even Josh thought he was killing himself.

His addiction shocked his wife, Katie, his family, his friends and all who knew him as the clean-cut, all-American kid. They said "If it could happen to Josh Hamilton, it could happen to anybody."[43]

Rehab at Granny's

Josh Hamilton hit bottom and struggled to recover in rehabilitation centers eight times. For a time he lost everything that mattered to him: his wife, children, parents, and baseball. In 2006, full of shame and tired of living a nightmare, he ended up on his granny's front porch at 2:15 am.

Hardly recognizing her six-foot-four grandson, his grandmother took him in, cleaned him up, fed him, and offered him a place to sleep. Soon he was following the "Granny Plan": no sleeping past 10:30 in the morning, eating at least three meals a day, going to bed at a decent hour, and no drugs.

Mary Holt, Josh's seventy-two-year-old granny, breathed positive thoughts into his life and reminded him that Granny knows best. She nurtured him with his favorite good ol' country food: bacon and eggs with grits, pork chops and biscuits with squash, steak and mashed potatoes with gravy. It seemed he was always eating.

One night Josh woke from a nightmare, covered in sweat. He couldn't shake the fear, so the big four-million-dollar baseball player knocked on his granny's bedroom door, opened it, and walked in.

"Slide over, Granny," he said. "I'm scared."[44]

As the drug haze cleared, he understood for the first time how much he had hurt the people he loved. On his knees, Josh cried out to God and asked for help. He didn't bargain with God or blame anyone else for his mistakes. Josh admitted his weakness and his addiction. He gave it all to God, knowing that his problems were too big for him to handle alone. As he flipped through a Bible, he came upon a verse that empowered him, James 4:7: "So humble yourself before God. Resist the devil and he will flee from you."[45]

Good days began to replace the bad. When cravings taunted Josh, he spoke his verse. When nightmares paralyzed him with fear, he spoke his verse. Josh walked the bumpy road to recovery one step at a time with God. Alone he couldn't win the battle, but with God he couldn't lose.

Thinking about his recovery, Josh now says, "It wasn't my timing, it was God's timing [for me] to get sober."[46]

Over time, Josh made peace with his family. Three months later when leaving Granny's house, Josh wrote to her, "People talk about tough love, but you showed me true love."[47]

MAJOR LEAGUES

Seven months later, the Devil Rays reinstated Josh Hamilton to play on a minor league team. In December 2006, he got his long-awaited second chance at his baseball career. The Chicago Cubs drafted him and then quickly traded him to the Cincinnati Reds. Josh Hamilton made his major league debut in April 2007 in a game between the Cincinnati Reds and the Chicago Cubs. Before he stepped up to the plate to bat, the crowd stood and cheered for him. Josh choked back his tears and took a minute to calm his emotions.

From his crouch position, Cubs catcher Michael Barrett looked up and said, "You deserve it, Josh. Take it all in, brother. I'm happy for you."[48]

The Texas Rangers signed him in 2008. From his first day with the Rangers, Josh felt right at home. The support and acceptance of his teammates strengthened him. Out of respect for Josh, his teammates even celebrated the 2010 playoff victories by showering him with ginger ale, not the usual champagne.

He won the hearts of fans with his talent and honesty about drug abuse. They voted him into the All-Star Games five years in a row, from 2008 to 2012, where he wowed them with his homerun-hitting prowess. Besides being named the ALCS MVP (American League Championship Series Most

Valuable Player), he was also voted the American League MVP and MLB.com Player of the Year in 2010.

Josh Hamilton never forgets that he lives with addiction. Someone travels with him to away games, and he carries no extra cash. According to Major League Baseball rules, he is tested for drugs three times per week. He feels no shame in these precautions but considers them part of the reality of being a recovering addict.

Every day, Josh Hamilton proves he is an overcomer. To battle his addiction, he humbles himself before God, admits his weakness, and asks for God's help. With an open and honest heart he faces each problem that comes his way.

A Bigger Purpose

During the dark days of her husband's addiction, Katie Hamilton predicted "You're going to be back playing baseball, because there's a bigger plan for you. When you come back, it's going to be about more than baseball."[49]

Josh now believes his purpose is to speak to others who need help, offer hope to the hopeless, and warn kids about the dangers of drugs. God gave him a second chance to use his talent at baseball for this bigger purpose.

Josh and Katie often share their story of God's grace and Christ's power in their lives. They speak after baseball games, at recovery centers, and at churches, lingering to answer all questions and sign all autographs. Josh warns his audience about drug addiction, "When you think it can't happen to you, it can."

He also hosts baseball camps for youth ages twelve to eighteen. He teaches them tips he learned in the Major Leagues about batting, fielding, and base running. More importantly, he talks to them about making good choices in life, learning from mistakes, and respecting their grannies.

Most recently the Hamiltons formed The Four Twelve Foundation (based on Hebrews 4:12), partnering with other ministries to serve and give to those in need in the US and around the world.

In 2008, Josh Hamilton published the book, *Beyond Belief: Finding the Strength to Come Back.* In writing his story, he wanted to connect with people struggling with addiction and give them hope. "It's a God-thing!" he says when asked about his journey back to baseball. "What I messed up, God is using for His glory now."

Notable Quotable

"What I messed up God is using for His glory now."
– Josh Hamilton

Points to Remember

- Ask for God's help.
- God provides a way out of temptation.
- Stay humble.
- Admit your weaknesses.
- Learn from your mistakes.

Take Action

1. Sometimes your problems may be too big for you to handle alone. Josh Hamilton turned to God for help when he failed to overcome his drug addiction on his own. Have you ever asked for God's help with your problems? How often are you willing to ask for his help?
2. Recall a time when God provided a way out of temptations that gripped you. What did you learn from that experience?
3. It would be easy for Josh Hamilton to be prideful about his baseball skills and his status as a Major League Baseball player, yet he remains humble before God. Where in your life do you need to be humble?
4. How does admitting your weaknesses help you conquer your problems?
5. What can you learn from past mistakes?

To Learn More about Josh Hamilton

His book (with Tim Keown): *Beyond Belief: finding the strength to come back* (New York: Faith Words, 2008).
His website: www.joshhamilton.net
The Los Angeles Angels of Anaheim: http://losangeles. angels.mlb.com
The Four Twelve Foundation: www.joshhamilton.net/fourt welve-foundation

End Notes

1 All quotes are from a telephone interview on October 30, 2013.
2 SEAL is an acronym meaning Sea, Air, Land.
3 Psalm 27:1, Holy Bible, New King James Version
4 Psalm 27:5,14, Holy Bible, New King James Version
5 The Gold Star symbolizes the loss and sacrifice of a military service member.
6 All quotes, except where noted, are from two personal interviews on August 10, 2010, and October 24, 2010, and one telephone interview on March 30, 2011.
7 Bob Mortimer, *Hope and Courage Across America*. (CreateSpace Independent Publishing Platform, 2011), p.361.
8 Mortimer, p.317
9 All quotes are from e-mail correspondence in August and September 2013.
10 Lisa Ann Hammond, *In Heaven We'll Be Free*. 1995. Used by permission.
11 Lisa Ann Hammond, *You Are the Song in Me*. 1996. Used by permission.
12 All quotes are from telephone interviews on July 29, 2010, and August 12, 2010.
13 Only 400 children and teens per year in the US are diagnosed with osteosarcoma.

[14] All quotes are from a telephone interview on June 19, 2014, unless otherwise noted.

[15] Phyllis Vavold, *Grace for the Raging Storm: A Story of God's Provision in the Midst of Tragedy and Loss* (Nampa, ID: Phyllis Vavold Ministries, 2012), p. 131.

[16] Vavold, p. 136

[17] Vavold, p. 79

[18] Vavold, pp.48, 50

[19] Vavold, p. 94

[20] Vavold, p. 134

[21] Vavold, p. 114

[22] Vavold, p. 126

[23] All quotes are from two telephone interviews on April 19, 2011, and May 4, 2011.

[24] Bernie Salazar's assistantship gave him money to pay for tuition in exchange for teaching duties.

[25] All quotes are from a personal interview on February 18, 2011.

[26] Isaiah 40: 28–31, New Living Translation

[27] All quotes are from a telephone interview on June 28, 2010 and September 2, 2014.

[28] All quotes are from an e-mail interview on February 29, 2012, unless otherwise noted.

[29] Gigi Murfitt, *Caregiver's Devotions to Go* (Orange, CA: Extreme Diva Media, Inc., 2010), p. 10.

[30] Murfitt, p. 18

[31] Murfitt, p. 21

[32] Murfitt, p. 140

[33] Gabe Murfitt, *My Message is C.L.E.A.R.: Hope and Strength in the Face of Life's Greatest Adversities* (Woodinville, WA: Gabriel's Foundation of Hope, 2012), p. 6.

[34] Murfitt, Gabe, p. 114

[35] Murfitt, Gigi, p. 73

36 Murfitt, Gabe, p. 81
37 Richard Durrett, "Rangers' Josh Hamilton wins AL MVP," *ESPN.com: Baseball* (November 23, 2010), accessed April 5, 2011.
38 Josh Hamilton, *Beyond Belief: Finding the Strength to Come Back,* (New York: Faith Words, 2008), p. 253.
39 Hamilton, p. 222
40 Hamilton, p. 3
41 Hamilton, p. 82
42 Hamilton, p. 134
43 Hamilton, p. 83
44 Hamilton, p. 166
45 James 4:7, New Living Translation
46 Quotes, unless otherwise noted, are from an informal talk that Josh Hamilton gave publically after a baseball game on March 29, 2009, in Surprise, Arizona.
47 Hamilton, p. 183
48 Hamilton, p. 218
49 Hamilton, p. 186

Made in the USA
Charleston, SC
03 April 2015